Thought Replacement Therapy

Cynthia Ann Hunt, LCSW

Copyright © 2008 by Cynthia Ann Hunt
First printing 2008

All rights reserved, including the right of reproduction, in whole or in part in any form.

Additional copies of this book can be ordered at
cynthialcsw@comcast.net

Designed by Compton Design Studio
bert@comptonds.com

ISBN: 978-0-615-20740-7

Printed in the United States of America
ACT Publishing, Salt Lake City, Utah

Thought Replacement Therapy

Cynthia Ann Hunt, LCSW

Bickersteth
Jan 2010

Contents

Acknowledgments vii

Introduction ix

The Other Side of Fear 1

AM/FM Stations 15

States of Consciousness—Celestial, Terrestrial, and Telestial ... 25

The Train from Shame to Recovery 37

How to Discern Healthy and Unhealthy Relationships 49

Our Relationships Mirror Our Relationship with God 59

Is There No Other Way? 73

Thought Replacement Therapy

The Gethsemane Map 79

Recognition of a Loss 91

"Let This Mind Be In You" 101

Celestial Rewards.. 113

A Gethsemane Moment.. 119

Thought Replacement Therapy 129

The Truth Will Set You Free 145

Real Truth.. 155

About The Author 165

Acknowledgments

The examples I've used in this book are real cases, with altered names and gender to protect the identity and preserve the privacy of my clients. I've also created composite characters and scenarios to further protect and maintain confidentiality.

I want to thank the numerous clients who have allowed me to be a small part of their lives as they have traversed through personal trials and sorrow. Thank you for the lessons taught and learned from this walk with you; I have grown to love you in a way and to a degree I never imagined possible when I began my career in counseling twenty years ago.

I also want to express my appreciations to Leslie Stitt, Helen Cram, and Shanna Francis who worked as editors. Thank you for your diligence, patience, and added inspiration.

Introduction

• •

Thought Replacement Therapy is a powerful innovative technique for influencing spiritual awareness. Every choice, action and thought is irreversibly predicated on a spiritual law that we are either keeping or not keeping in the moment.

I believe there are three states of consciousness—celestial, terrestrial, and telestial—and, that, at various times, we each find ourselves in all three levels or degrees of consciousness. Each degree can instill greater humility and wisdom, leading us one step closer to a higher level of consciousness.

I wanted to present this information in book form to help people learn how to do the following:

1. Replace telestial thoughts and actions with terrestrial and celestial thoughts and actions.

2. Resolve inner conflict by discovering powerful spiritual principles that influence the way we think and act.
3. Recapture our mind where we will gain freedom from thoughts that hold us captive.

I have been compiling notes for this work over the past ten years and know the thoughts that developed in preparation for this work were spiritually inspired.

CHAPTER 1
The Other Side of Fear

....

Hidden deep within each of us is a type of spiritual prison in our mind where painful memories, beliefs, and even harmful self-deceptions or lies are locked away. Circumstances or events can open this locked and well-secured portion of our mind. When the unconscious spills into conscious awareness, and the spirit prison of our mind opens, we can be infused by negative childhood or life memories and beliefs. We stand at a crossroad where our past, present, and future meet.

At this crossroad, we face three choices. First, we can suppress these debilitating thoughts and deceptions, quickly locking them back into the spirit prison of our mind. By doing so, we temporarily protect ourselves against the anxiety caused by these thoughts. Denial is a powerful type of lie used to suppress thoughts, keeping them imprisoned deep within us; it is a tool used to create a false sense of safety and to avoid taking responsibility for our lives.

Our second choice at the crossroad is to allow negative memories and beliefs to control our present and future choices. We accept the lies and deceptions, enabling them to continue hurting our lives. The consequence of this choice is the continuance of a life filled with fear and anxiety, which inhibits personal growth, love of God, and love of others. Toxic memories, deceptions, and lies originate from Satan. He is the author of all lies, and most fear stems from believing his insidious lies.

Lies keep us from our future and bind us to our past—and to our pain. Satan continues his influence over us, enabling fear to control our lives. When we believe a lie, we become numb to the conscious real world of truth, love, and growth and fall spiritually asleep. At this point, we must concede that the adversary has control and influence over our thought processes, or we must suffer future consequences.

Our third choice at the crossroad is to allow ourselves to challenge false beliefs and old memories, thus changing the course of our lives and, intrinsically, our character and even our personalities. This becomes an opportunity to begin a cleansing process. This is a spiritual process where old, tired memories and false beliefs are dispelled, thus eliminating the power and influence they have in our lives.

"For God, who commanded the light to shine out of darkness, hath shined in our hearts, to give the light of the knowledge of the glory of God . . . . For our light affliction, which is but for a moment, worketh for us a far more exceeding and eternal weight of glory." (II Corinthians 4:6, 17)

Becoming Spiritually Minded

One way to challenge old beliefs and painful memories is to decide to love and honor God rather than to please man. We must step out of our numb, unconscious, temporal zone and enter the spiritual mind. This decision and subsequent cleansing is what I call the Gethsemane Process. When we are spiritually minded, all manner of light, truth, and peace can be obtained.

Reflecting upon your life, consider what you may have to sacrifice in order to become spiritually minded. Are you willing to relinquish false pride, lies, greed, fear, temporal aspirations, addictions, and/or old resentments? Are you willing to face your fears and overcome them through faith and truth?

Here are some ways we block the truth from entering our lives:

Self-Justification

I remember, years ago, the day I resolved to give up chocolate. The very next morning I went to work only to find a tray of doughnuts in the break room. Of course, they were chocolate doughnuts to tempt and try my resolve! I looked away and went into my office. But, all I could think about were the chocolate doughnuts beckoning to me. Quickly forming a lie to justify my plan of action, I told myself it would be okay to eat just half a doughnut; think how much discipline I would be exercising to do so, and how many calories I would be eliminating!

I re-entered the break room, cut a doughnut in half, ate it, and, with my plan for giving up chocolate compromised, went back to my desk. I then continued to rationalize and lie to myself by telling myself how "lonely" the other half of the doughnut looked sitting there with all the whole doughnuts around it. By believing this lie, I gave myself permission to return to the break room and consume the other half of the doughnut. But, of course, this isn't the end of the story; once I had dishonored myself and entered the realm of the temporal mind, I set myself up for eating more and more doughnuts—almost the entire tray of them! Afterward, I realized I had believed a lie to justify my actions.

Self-Deception

A young woman named Anne left for a church-proselyting mission. After only a few months, she decided that she should return home. She believed her family needed her and that God didn't really want her to be on a mission. However, in truth, Anne was experiencing some anxieties that were not related to her concern for her family. Instead of pushing through her fears and feelings of inadequacy, she chose a self-deceiving option—to return home. This began to reduce her immediate anxieties and fears. However, upon returning home, Anne went into a deep depression that lasted almost two years.

Anne would never admit that, perhaps, it was a mistake to go home prematurely and that she wouldn't be suffering from clinical depression had she stayed and worked through her anxieties and fears. Consequently, this self-deception changed the course of her life and contributed to a depressive illness.

Obsessions

Diane was attracted to a too-good-to-be-true, "get-rich-quick" scheme. One common thread runs through this type of deception, and many others like it—a time element. "You have to purchase now, or you will forever lose the opportunity."

Diane had fallen for this type of scheme numerous times before, and frequently had convinced others to participate. Usually, within the first twenty four to forty eight hours of being taken advantage of in this way, a person becomes aware of the truth. In fact, many states have "Buyer's Remorse" laws that allow people the opportunity to rethink a decision. However, Diane chose to continue believing the lies, trying to garner support for her false beliefs by convincing others. This problem brought financial ruin to her, as well as to those she influenced. By believing lies and trying to convince others to buy into the lies, false beliefs became obsessions.

Passing on Fears

I have always had a fear of mice. When I discovered that my kitchen had been plagued with the vile rodent, I decided to completely remodel in a feeble attempt to eradicate the object of my fear. Not long afterward, my daughter, just a toddler at the time, came into the den and fearlessly informed me, "Mommy, there is a mouse in the kitchen."

I said, "No, honey, I remodeled the whole kitchen; there are no mice in this house." She insisted there was a mouse in the kitchen. To humor her, I went into the kitchen. Sure enough, there was a mouse standing on its hind legs, scratching at the sliding glass door trying to get out. I immediately did what any responsible parent would do—I jumped up on the dining room table and began screaming at the top of my lungs.

My little girl looked up at me with wide eyes and in a fearful voice asked me, "Mommy, it's going to kill us, isn't it?"

I rather hysterically assured her, "No honey, not me, because I am up here on the table!"

I realize this is a humorous story; however, looking back, it demonstrates how big and real a lie can be in our lives. My intense fear of mice was reinforced by my behavior, and the fear was needlessly passed on to my daughter.

Projection

Sometimes our lies are projected onto others. Instead of asking God to help us identify and overcome our own weaknesses and shortcomings, we spend an enormous amount of time and energy trying to "fix" others. For example, Margie wants her husband to take a more active role at church because she struggles with her own spirituality. When we fail to reach our own spiritual potential, we may become addicted to another's by involving ourselves in helping them reach what we believe their potential should be.

False Pride

Consider the common fear of public speaking. The underlying thoughts accompanying this fear are typically about how we will appear to others—how others will judge us. Most of the anxiety stems from anticipation; people create a false negative reality. We tell ourselves that our fears will be apparent and we will look inadequate, vulnerable, and/or make mistakes and be viewed as unintelligent. Some of these thoughts may stem from childhood experiences where we made mistakes or performed less than perfectly and received criticism from others or from ourselves. Such thoughts are generated from a sense of false pride—a belief that we need to live up to an image of perfection, intelligence, and/or importance.

Lack of Abundance

Many self-deceptions and lies relate to money. Ron feels financially insecure and worries that he is not going to be able to earn enough money. He also worries about not having enough money for retirement. Then Ron begins to obsess so much about earning and saving money that his obsession begins to negatively impact his life. Ron's fear of a lack of abundance is never satiated. Love of God and others often becomes secondary to his obsession to earn more money. This fear-based life may generate temporal gain, but, ultimately, the fruit it produces—selfishness, insecurity, shortsightedness, false pride, and even greed—is bitter, indeed.

Overprotection

Many parents experience a fear that their children may make poor choices and mistakes that could ruin their future lives. As a result of this fear, parents unwittingly begin to overprotect, rescue, and, ironically, even enable their children in their mistakes. By protecting and shielding their children from the opportunities to learn and grow from the consequences of their actions, they deprive them of the essential knowledge and experience gleaned from these critical life lessons.

This type of parenting diminishes both the parents' and their children's self-esteem. The parents' fear continues to generate more fear as a self-fulfilling prophecy is developed and fulfilled. The children fail to learn appropriate life lessons, while the parents succeed at believing they are inadequate parents. In this downward spiraling scenario, the parents increase their efforts to overprotect their misbehaving children, while the children become increasingly out of control.

Immediate Gratification

Pamela, who came from a great family, left a healthy marital relationship. What motivated this decision? In a weakened spiritual condition, she may have been vulnerable and felt "trapped" in a relationship with someone she thought she no longer loved. She may have believed she needed to get out of the relationship so she could become "her own person and be herself." She may even have believed there was someone else better suited to her personality. Because we live in a "fast-food," obsolescent society, Pamela wanted immediate happiness, fulfillment, and bliss without much effort. As she fell further and further away from spirit and truth, she became more and more convinced of the veracity of the lies. Because of the lies and fears swirling around within her mind, she became totally convinced that she should leave a good relationship. This prolonged state of mind eventually took her out of her marriage and even out of her church.

This critical life-altering action was rooted in a small incipient lie—a slow, subtle, and powerful erroneous idea regarding her marital situation and the resultant fears associated with staying in the relationship.

Insecurity

In contrast to reasonably healthy marriages that sometimes disintegrate, some very abusive relationships live on and on at the expense of one, or both, of the partners. In marriages where abuse is common, fears enable the abuse to continue. Many remain in difficult marriages because they fear being alone after a divorce or they may fear negative public opinion. Some doubt their own abilities to survive without the abusive partner. They fear they may disappoint God by breaking their marital covenants; consequently, their faith in God's everlasting love and concern for them flickers and dims. Both the abused and the abuser become caught in an ugly web of lies and fear.

As lies and fear develop, sin always follows. When this pattern continues day after day, week after week, month after month, and perhaps year after year, the lies and sins become enmeshed tighter and tighter with the person's identity. Even though most lies remain subtly hidden and unnoticed, they continue to influence behavior.

The Fear and Faith Triangles

When individuals begin believing the lies that create fear—fear of not getting what they want, fear of loss, fear of rejection, fear of real or perceived threats, or any other fear—they usually kick into a control mode, which is a very ineffective survival mechanism. When people realize they cannot control other people, places, and things, they become angry, irritable, restless, frustrated, discontented, or even depressed. Sometimes when people experience these negative feelings, they try to self-medicate with addictive behaviors. I have never had anyone tell me, "I felt so spiritual I decided to enhance the feelings at the corner liquor store." Whenever you are angry ask yourself, "What am I trying to control and can I control it?" Also ask yourself, "What am I afraid of?"

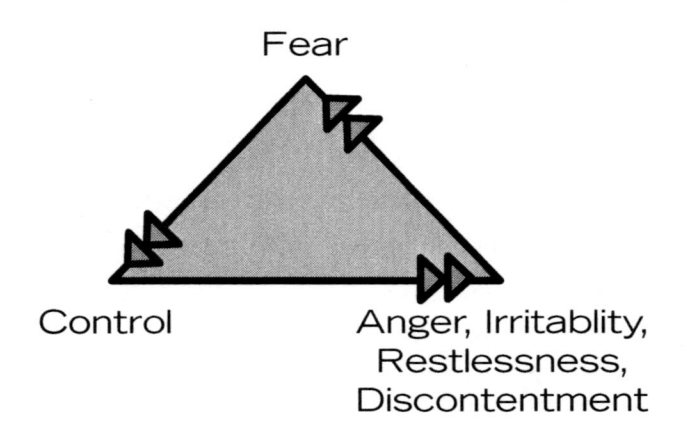

Fear

Control   Anger, Irritablity,
                 Restlessness,
                 Discontentment

The opposite of fear is faith—trusting in God and surrendering our will to His. This allows us to peacefully relinquish our efforts to control our environment and others. The resulting feelings—

in contrast to those felt in the fear mode—are love, peace, and serenity.

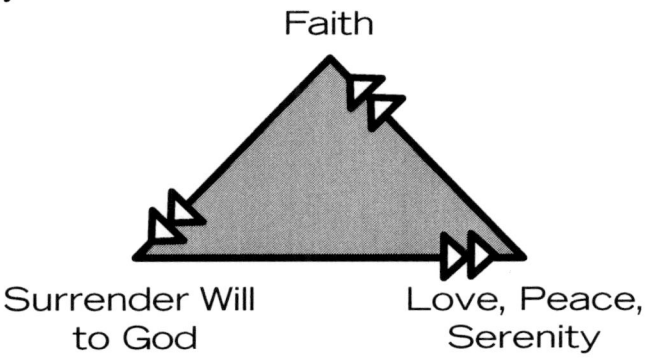

```
            Faith
             /\
            /  \
           /    \
          /      \
         /        \
        /_____\
Surrender Will   Love, Peace,
   to God         Serenity
```

People Run on Faith or Fear

We can replace fear by turning to God and praying for greater faith. Just like the choices we have when it comes to filling our gas tanks with different grades or quality of gasoline, we can fill our spiritual tanks with varying levels or degrees of faith. The more we exercise faith, the purer our faith becomes; the purer the grade of faith, the more smoothly our lives will run.

Maintenance is also a critical part of keeping our lives running smoothly. Make a list of actions that fill your faith tank and those that fill your fear tank. The following are a few examples.

Actions that Fill the Fear Tank:

- Assuming—do you *really* know what others are thinking or what will happen in the future?
- Comparing yourself with others.
- All-or-nothing thinking.

- Wanting other people to be different from who they really are.
- Not accepting life on life's terms.
- Breaking commandments.
- Believing lies.
- Holding onto resentment(s).
- Worrying about what others think.
- Competing.
- Relying on your own intelligence.
- Masking pain with food, alcohol, drugs, pornography, sex, shopping, etc.
- Stretching the truth to get your own way.
- Being unwilling to let go.

Warning! Please note that if your fear tank is more than 50 percent full, do not make any critical decisions; your judgment may be impaired. Also, never enter a relationship out of fear and never leave a relationship out of fear, unless the relationship is abusive or destructive.

Actions that Fill our Faith Tank:

- Praying sincerely.
- Accepting others.
- Forgiving others.
- Making positive affirmations.
- Surrendering your will to God's.
- Studying scriptures.
- Serving others.

- Worshiping God at church and in daily life.
- Keeping the Sabbath day holy.
- Making and keeping commitments.
- Keeping the commandments.
- Feeling the fear but doing what's right anyway.

Attention! Please note that keeping your faith tank more than 50 percent full will lead to a greater love of God, self, and others, which will heighten your better judgment.

If You Want to Change a Behavior, Break a Secret

Larry had inappropriate thoughts about a woman in his congregation, during church. These were quickly followed by another thought: he should tell his wife about his improper thoughts. He immediately began to rationalize all the reasons he shouldn't tell her—it would hurt her self-esteem, besides, the thoughts would never go any further and, most likely, her reaction would be unpleasant, etc.

He wrestled with his reasoning, but he finally followed the prompting to tell the truth. With great difficulty and shame, he told his wife and, of course, her reaction was exactly what he thought it would be. She was hurt and felt betrayed by him. Later, however, Larry related that his choice to expose these thoughts had helped him overcome similar thoughts he encountered soon afterward; this ultimately drew him closer to his wife, who had grown to respect him as she noticed his more refined character and increased level of spirituality.

How often do we sacrifice faith for fear? Do we begin to dwell on the "what ifs" and falter? Do we drown in the distractions of the world, or do we maintain our focus? Like those with Attention Deficit Disorders, it is often difficult for us to keep our mind on the mark when distracted by the cares and burdens of the world. Faith is the antithesis of fear; faith cannot prevail when fear is present. We cannot go over, under, or around fear, but, as we walk through fear, with faith, it can take us to a higher level of truth and inspiration. Each time irrational fear based on lies is conquered, we become stronger spiritually.

CHAPTER 2
AM/FM Stations

....

All problems, struggles, and despair originate within the frequency of the temporal/fear mind, whereas, all solutions are found within the spiritual mind. This life is the time to learn how to think correctly—with the spiritual mind.

There are many voices in the world. Do we choose to listen to temporal/fear voices or do we choose to heed the spiritual voices? How do we know which voice we are listening to? To which "station" do you subscribe? It is critical that we choose the correct frequency, because our peace of mind depends upon it.

Let's use the analogy that God is the God of the spiritual mind and Satan is the god of the temporal/fear mind. We'll say the spiritual mind is governed by truth and the temporal/fear mind is governed by lies. Further, let's use the metaphor of the AM/FM stations to describe different life frequencies.

In your temporal mind, life controls you. Once you betray or break a commitment or commandment, or lie to yourself or to someone else, you immediately move into your temporal mind. In your spiritual mind, you give control of your life, and everyone else's, to God. In your temporal mind, you try to control your life and everyone else's. In your spiritual mind, you surrender your thoughts to God. When you are in your spiritual mind, you cannot be hurt or offended because you receive your self-worth and self-love from God.

Is it possible that in the Millennium, Satan will not be bound by whips or chains, but only by our thoughts? Now is the time to learn how to think. The war between the heaven/hell portion of our mind is about truth and lies.

Within each mind there is the possibility of a heaven or a hell. Hell in the mind is created by not accepting life on God's terms— by not accepting His plan. We "kick against the pricks" so to speak, always wanting life to be different from how it is.

In contrast, heaven in the mind is accepting life on God's terms and accepting His will. Remember, all of our experiences and challenges are placed before us to strengthen and refine us.

The following principles illustrate the importance of choosing correct "life frequencies."

AM & FM Frequencies of the Mind

All AM stations use Anger/Fear Mind frequencies that generate negative feelings, such as irritability, restlessness, and discontent. Within each of these frequencies we can find our own hell. We can go from AM100 to AM1000—from mild anxiety, to panic attacks, to life threatening depression, depending on the duration and intensity of our thoughts and feelings. The definition of the hell portion is being self-willed, which results in wanting people or situations to be different from how they really are, and refusing to accept life on life's terms.

In contrast, we can also tune into FM Faith Mind frequencies where we can select any station from FM100 to FM1000. Within each of these frequencies we find love, peace, and serenity. We do this by trusting in God and working to stay spiritually tuned to the heaven portion of our mind. This is important because we can make correct and lasting choices only in our spiritual mind. The definition of living in the heavenly portion of our mind is accepting life on life's terms, or surrendering our will to God's will.

Characteristics of the AM Anger/Fear Mind And the FM Faith Mind Station

The AM Anger/Fear Mind station

- Believes lies.
- Lacks judgment.
- Is self-centered and selfish.
- Is prideful.
- Has low self-esteem and self-worth based on belief of what others think.
- Uses self-talk such as, "Give me a break," or "Why, why, why?"
- Has feelings of being "stuck."

Thought Replacement Therapy

- Fights going to church or doing anything of a spiritual nature.
- Doesn't forgive and holds onto resentment.
- Loves power and tries to control others.
- Is inconsistent.
- Has all-or-nothing thought processes.
- Is controlled by emotions.
- Has obsessive compulsive thought patterns.
- Is beset by addictions.
- Suffers from trust issues.
- Frequently compares self with others.
- Acts out of fear, not faith.

The FM Faith Mind Station

- Believes truth.
- Gives selfless service.
- Humbles self.
- Depends on God for self-esteem and self-worth.
- Knows that with God all things work together for good.
- Gives gratitude for trials, understanding that trials are learning experiences.
- Allows freedom for self and others.
- Doubts not, fears not.
- Enjoys going to church.
- Is filled with charity and forgiveness.
- Keeps promises, commitments, and commandments.
- Is sincere.
- Is sensitive to the needs of others.

- Trusts God.
- Surrenders thoughts to God.
- Gains a conscious victory over self/appetites.
- Wants to please God rather than man.
- Continues to grow and progress, always choosing the highest good.
- Hungers and thirsts after righteousness.

Which signal are you tuned into most frequently? Believing lies causes enormous self-doubt and self-deception and inflicts pain multigenerationally. When we believe a lie, it is like falling asleep in the conscious, real world and waking up in the unconscious, unreal world ruled by the adversary. Truth is the key that unlocks the mind and reduces the AM volume.

These principles are taught in the following story:

Lies Buried Alive

It was late and Jon couldn't sleep, so he decided to catch up on overdue projects from work. He wasn't at the computer very long when a powerful negative thought began to take control of his mind. He later admitted he had felt tired, lonely, stressed, and overwhelmed with work when, suddenly, almost without warning, he escaped into the world of pornography. Many subtle lies catapulted him into this hypnotic, dream-like state of mind and a few minutes of counterfeit pleasure turned into days, weeks, and months of emotional and spiritual pain.

When Jon first chose to view pornography, he denied that

he was opening his mind and home to the adversary. Later, he admitted he had relinquished his mind to counterfeit sources of pleasure and happiness.

Are we spiritually connected by an invisible thread? Do our actions affect others? A few weeks after Jon started viewing pornography, his wife, unaware of Jon's problem, began to have an inappropriate relationship with a co-worker. Around this same time, their daughter, who always seemed to reflect the family's pain, began a sexual relationship with her boyfriend.

The subtle lies Jon believed included: "No one will ever know," "Just this once won't matter," and, "I'm not hurting anyone else." However, Jon's conscience began to bother him. He could have buried the lies alive through denial or, perhaps, anti-depressants or anti-anxiety medication to numb the pain. But, because Jon was sensitive to the spirit, he was prompted to confess his problem. Coincidentally, his wife and daughter confessed their indiscretions shortly afterwards. Later, in counseling, the family recognized how their separate choices were linked spiritually.

As this family learned, the remedy for guilt, shame, and emotional pain is found only in repentance, forgiveness, and truth. Satan is the author of fear. Most fears stem from believing lies that keep us from our future and bind us to our shame. When you find the lie and expose it, you can be set free. As the scriptures promise, *"The truth shall make you free." (John 8:32)* I believe that if you never told a lie you would never have an addiction. All of our problems originate in a temporal realm, and all of the solutions are found within the spiritual realm.

How do we recapture our thoughts and move from an AM

frequency to an FM frequency? The following is the beginning of the road map that provides for this spiritual journey.

AM Station Thoughts Destroy You

Keep track of each thought and action that brings you into the AM station. How do you turn the volume up on the AM station and down on the FM station?

"What ifs," "I can't," and "if only" turn up the AM volume.
- Why can't I be more confident?
- If only I could change.
- Why can't I forgive myself?
- What if I try and fail?
- Why can't he or she accept me?

FM Station Thoughts Heal You

How do you turn the volume up on the FM station and down on the AM station?

Counter the AM thoughts with FM thoughts. Keep track of the thoughts that bring you into the FM station. Here are some examples.
- It is none of my business what others think of me.
- I am okay even if I make a mistake.
- I believed a lie and now I have to tell someone the truth.
- It takes time to heal, and that's okay.
- I can have a problem and still be all right.
- With God's help I can achieve my goals.

Thought Replacement Therapy

Characteristics of the Temporal (AM) Mind and Spiritual (FM) Mind

AM STATION Temporal	FM STATION Spiritual
Sacrifices God's will for own	Sacrifices own will for God's
Compelled to please self and others	Compelled to please God
Tries to control all situations	Lets go and lets God
Denies God's laws	Obeys God's laws
Seeks instant gratification	Offers eternal gratitude
May try to give up life for others, or demand that others sacrifice for him or her	Accepts Christ's sacrifice and humbly and meekly allows others their free agency
Tries to take away others' pain and growth experiences	Turns to God to heal pain
Loves conditionally	Offers unconditional love
Seeks the honors and praises of men	Willing to suffer rejection, humiliation, persecution, and pain
Denies true feelings	Honors true feelings
Harbors resentment	Forgives easily
Victim mentality—believes others cause his or her pain and wants others to rely on him or her	Survivor mentality—relies on God and subdues pride

How to turn the volume up or down on the AM and FM stations:

AM STATION Temporal	FM STATION Spiritual
Resentment	Repent, forgive self & others
Anger/fear	Faith
Control/sin	Surrender will to God
Self-esteem based on the opinions of others	Self-esteem based on close relationship with God
Guilt/shame	Peace, love, joy, serenity
Addictions/at-one-ment with the world	At-one-ment with God
Negative thoughts	Prayer/scriptures
Pride	Humility
Blame	Accountability and responsibility

CHAPTER 3
States of Consciousness— Celestial, Terrestrial, and Telestial

....

In this world, each of us lives in varying states of consciousness. Inside each of us there are different degrees of glory and light. In I Corinthians, these degrees are compared to the sun, the moon, and the stars; they are named celestial (sun), terrestrial (moon), and telestial (stars). *(I Corinthians 15:41)* Like the varying amounts of light reflected from each heavenly body, the three degrees of glory also carry with them varying degrees of truth and light.

In the celestial state of consciousness, we believe truth; in a terrestrial state of consciousness, we believe truth mingled with lies; and in a telestial state of consciousness, much, or most of what we believe is based on lies to the extent that there is very little light, and much darkness. Each of these states of consciousness has different degrees of truth and lies that impact our lives accordingly for good or bad.

Multigenerational Truth and Lies

Everyone sees life through different filters. These filters come from our family of origin, close and distant ancestors, as well as our life experiences. Filters based on truth and lies continue to influence family members and loved ones as they are passed down from one generation to the next. These patterns often manifest themselves through deeply ingrained beliefs, habits, behaviors, and traditions.

From earth's "first brothers," we learn of the horrific result of the relationship between Cain and Abel. Cain slew his brother Abel. What lies did Cain believe that led to this event? Was Cain jealous of Abel? Did Cain compare himself to Abel? Did Cain compete with Abel? Did Cain feel entitled to blessings he did not earn? Ultimately, Cain believed the lie that he could win it all if he killed Abel, even though the resulting prize was a counterfeit.

From the beginning, many tragic stories of sibling rivalry have unfolded as a result of lies and the resulting sins. Sometimes the transgression is perpetrated against a child at the hands of a parent and not a sibling; or it may be against a parent at the hands of a child. The combinations are almost limitless; multigenerational lies can take on a myriad of forms. This family pain, and the deep-seated wounds associated with it, is often perpetuated through many generations because the pattern can be halted only by exposing the lie and accepting the truth.

Celestial Relationships

In celestial relationships, husbands and wives set boundaries and are honest with each other. There is a high degree of trust within the relationship, and they can count on one another to keep their commitments. They feel empathy and warmth for each other. This couple puts God first in their relationship, and neither is easily offended by the other. They care what their partner thinks of them; however, they derive their self-esteem primarily from God, not man. They are also supportive watchmen for one another.

People who primarily live in a celestial state of consciousness generally demonstrate the following characteristics or qualities:

1. Believe truth.
2. Fear God.
3. Execute righteous judgment.
4. Seek to overcome the world.
5. Live by faith.
6. Seek to see all things spiritually.
7. Make and keep commitments.
8. Live obedient to God's commandments.
9. Embrace reality from an eternal perspective.
10. Deny temporal desires and resist the temptations of the world.
11. Receive self-esteem based on relationship with God.
12. Have a great capacity to love.

Terrestrial Relationships

In terrestrial relationships, different degrees of truth are mingled with lies. Individuals feel pretty good about themselves most of the time. When they have a bad day, they regain their self-confidence from God—and others. In a terrestrial relationship the general attitude is, "He or she makes me feel good about myself," "I keep commitments when it is convenient," "sometimes I tell lies because I don't want to hurt someone." Or, depending upon the circumstances and/or self-motives, those in a terrestrial state may manipulate others to get what they want or need.

People who primarily live in a terrestrial state of consciousness generally demonstrate the following characteristics or qualities:

1. Rely on truth mingled with lies.
2. Fear God and man.
3. Execute righteous and unrighteous judgment.
4. Overcome the world at times, but are also, frequently, overcome by the world.
5. Act based on a faith/fear mix.
6. See both temporally and spiritually.
7. Usually keep commitments.
8. Usually keep God's commandments.
9. Live both in and out of reality.
10. Seek temporal and spiritual desires.
11. Receive self-esteem based on relationships with God and other people.
12. Fall in and out of love.

Telestial Relationships

In the telestial state of consciousness, people cannot see clearly through the filter of their mind. Anyone associated with people living in this state of consciousness is frequently worried about offending them. People may have to walk on egg shells when around this type of person. One cannot talk about anything important because they have an irrational thought process. They have no ability to discern truth, and when things go wrong, they frequently blame everyone else. They will make a statement, and when the statement is repeated back to them, they will firmly deny that they ever said it.

People in a telestial state of consciousness believe the whole world is out to get them, or that the whole world revolves around them. They usually have few friends and no deep or lasting relationships. They have little or no hope, reasoning ability, or capacity for truth. The filter in their mind that is designed to keep out lies grows weaker and weaker until the lines between lies and truth become blurred. These individuals' spiritual filters become dimmer and dimmer the more they try to control others.

Individuals living in a telestial state of consciousness may sometimes suppress feelings of inadequacy by mitigating the pain with alcohol and/or other mind-altering substances. Or, they may adopt obsessive-compulsive behavior in such areas as shopping, working, cleaning, or eating. People who say or think they are spiritual, but are controlled by these negative characteristics, may not be living in reality or peace.

In a telestial relationship, each party experiences good feelings that stem from being liked by the other: One partner may say, "I am nothing without your approval." There may also be a fatal attraction. The general attitude is, "I'll tell you whatever it takes to make you love me." Another partner might say, "I can't live without you; in fact, I'm nothing without you and you're nothing without me."

In this relationship, the partners are held hostage by each other's neediness. Their relationship always comes before their relationship with God. It is a chameleon-type of relationship; a person may try to be whatever the other needs him or her to be. But when people put any relationship before God, they will end up losing it. *"I the Lord thy God am a jealous God . . ." "Thou shalt have no other gods before me." (Exodus 20:3,5)*

However, if, or when, they happen to give more control back to God, their filter becomes brighter. *"In whom the god of this world hath blinded the minds of them which believe not, lest the light of the glorious gospel of Christ, who is the image of God, should shine unto them." (II Corinthians 4:4)*

Those who primarily live in a telestial state of consciousness generally demonstrate the following characteristics or qualities:

1. Believe lies and tell lies.
2. Act, and react, motivated by fear of man.
3. Execute unrighteous judgment.
4. Are overcome by the world.
5. Are blinded by fear and lies.
6. Break commitments without conscience or remorse.
7. Break commandments.
8. Are unable to comprehend reality.
9. Deny spiritual and seek temporal desires.

10. Continually rewrite history for their own benefit.
11. Receive self-esteem based on relationships with other people.
12. Have little or no capacity to love.

Relationships within Degrees of Consciousness

As previously stated, each of us attains a different degree of light and truth—a light previously likened to the light reflected from the varying heavenly bodies: the sun, moon, and stars. These varying degrees of light affect our relations with our family members and various associates. For instance, parents who have grown to a spiritual degree likened to that of the sun—a celestial body—lead by this heightened example. They are emotionally balanced and available to family and friends. People in a celestial state of consciousness can serve as a type of watchman for their loved ones—they are emotionally, spiritually, mentally, and physically available when needed. People in a celestial state of consciousness are trustworthy. They guide with truth and light, and they have a great capacity to love and care for others. They strive to grow closer to God..

When a person living in a celestial state of consciousness marries another who is living in a celestial state of consciousness, or reality, their relationship grows closer in direct proportion to the degree they draw closer to God.

But, when a person living primarily in a celestial or terrestrial state of consciousness marries someone living in a telestial state of consciousness, the couple is divided by an emotional and spiritual gulf. Marriages that are split between different states of consciousness are based on different levels of truth. Soon after marrying a person in a different state of consciousness, one or both of the partners begin to realize they are unequally yoked. *"Be ye not unequally yoked together with unbelievers: for what fellowship hath righteousness with unrighteousness? And what communion hath light with darkness?" (II Corinthians 6:14)* Whatever separates individuals or couples from God, will also separate them in their relationship. For example, if money, food, alcohol, sex, etc. separate people from God, it will also separate people in a relationship.

Sometimes a couple will begin their relationship in similar states of consciousness, but, one, or the other, will grow into a higher degree of light above that of the person who stays stuck in a lower state. The partner with a higher degree of light may be continually drawn down into the other partner's dimmer state of consciousness in order to stay connected in the relationship. Thus, the relationship may come to feel like a marital prison. This scenario can also be applied to other personal relationships, such as parent/child, child/parent, friend/friend, coworker/coworker, etc.

A person in a terrestrial state of consciousness usually traverses between varying degrees of light and darkness at various times or in different situations in their lives, causing inconsistencies in their behavior. At times they may reflect qualities of a person living in a celestial state of consciousness; at other times, they may sink below, reflecting the characteristics of a person imprisoned in a telestial state of consciousness.

In a telestial state of consciousness, an individual's primary characteristics reflect the temporal world, in which lives are based more on lies than on truth. When confronted with truth, they react in varied telestial ways, because they care more about themselves than others. They shut themselves off from relationships, suffering from depression or addictions. They blame others for not respecting them and for creating their problems. In a telestial state, people often seek revenge, honoring the things of the temporal world, their god is in the image of themselves, other people, or the material things of this world.

Since they are usually insecure, these people often infringe on others' agency through controlling and irrational behavior. One cannot reason with a person living in a telestial state of consciousness. A person in this state of consciousness rewards evil for good and good for evil. No matter how hard others try to please this person or to make him or her happy, they will fail; everything they do will be "wrong." Often, charismatic telestial individuals may be loved and respected by those who know them on a superficial level, while projecting guilt, shame, and abuse on those closest to them. They have two faces: the one they show to others—the veneer; and the other, which is often exposed only to those closest to them.

In a telestial state, people often try to run others' lives, or, alternatively, they may be indifferent, uncaring, and insensitive. A relationship formed and maintained in this realm cannot survive, at least not in a healthy manner. People in a telestial state of consciousness are destroyers—not builders or creators. Also, they cannot be trusted as watchmen for others. Frequently, they make others their higher power and become enmeshed in relationships. Their self-esteem and self-worth are not God-based, but rather based on how they think others will perceive them.

Living Among Degrees of Consciousness

"Giving thanks unto the Father, which hath made us meet to be partakers of the inheritance of the saints in light: Who hath delivered us from the power of darkness, and hath translated us into the Kingdom of his dear Son." (Colossians 1:12-13)

In this life, all people live in different levels of truth or reality. There are those who are being raised by a parent who lives in the telestial state of consciousness or have a sibling who at times sees life through a dimly lit filter. Perhaps they have a supervisor, co-worker, spouse, or child who lives in a telestial state of consciousness.

As mentioned previously, the primary factor that affects the filter in our mind includes:

1. Deeply ingrained beliefs, habits, patterns, and behaviors that are passed down multigenerationally.
2. Life experiences or imprints.
3. Honesty with self and others.
4. Keeping commandments and commitments.
5. Medication.
6. Fostering a closer relationship with God.

It is often challenging for those living in a higher state of consciousness to live and work in a temporal world with those who play the game of life according to a lower state of consciousness with little or no moral standards. Since those living in a telestial state of mind are often incapable of being honest with themselves or others, it may appear that the team with limited rules has all the advantages of this world—and they often do. On the other hand, the telestial crown or trophy is hollow, and provides little to no genuine fulfillment or contentment. Thus, the bearer continues his or her mad search for that which does not, and cannot, satisfy.

The filters of those living in the various degrees of consciousness are as different as the sun, the moon, and the stars. While living in the temporal world, we may spend our lives traveling among the three different states of consciousness depending upon our choices and beliefs. But in the end, the dominant state of consciousness we embrace in this life will follow us into the next.

Thought Replacement Therapy

States of Consciousness

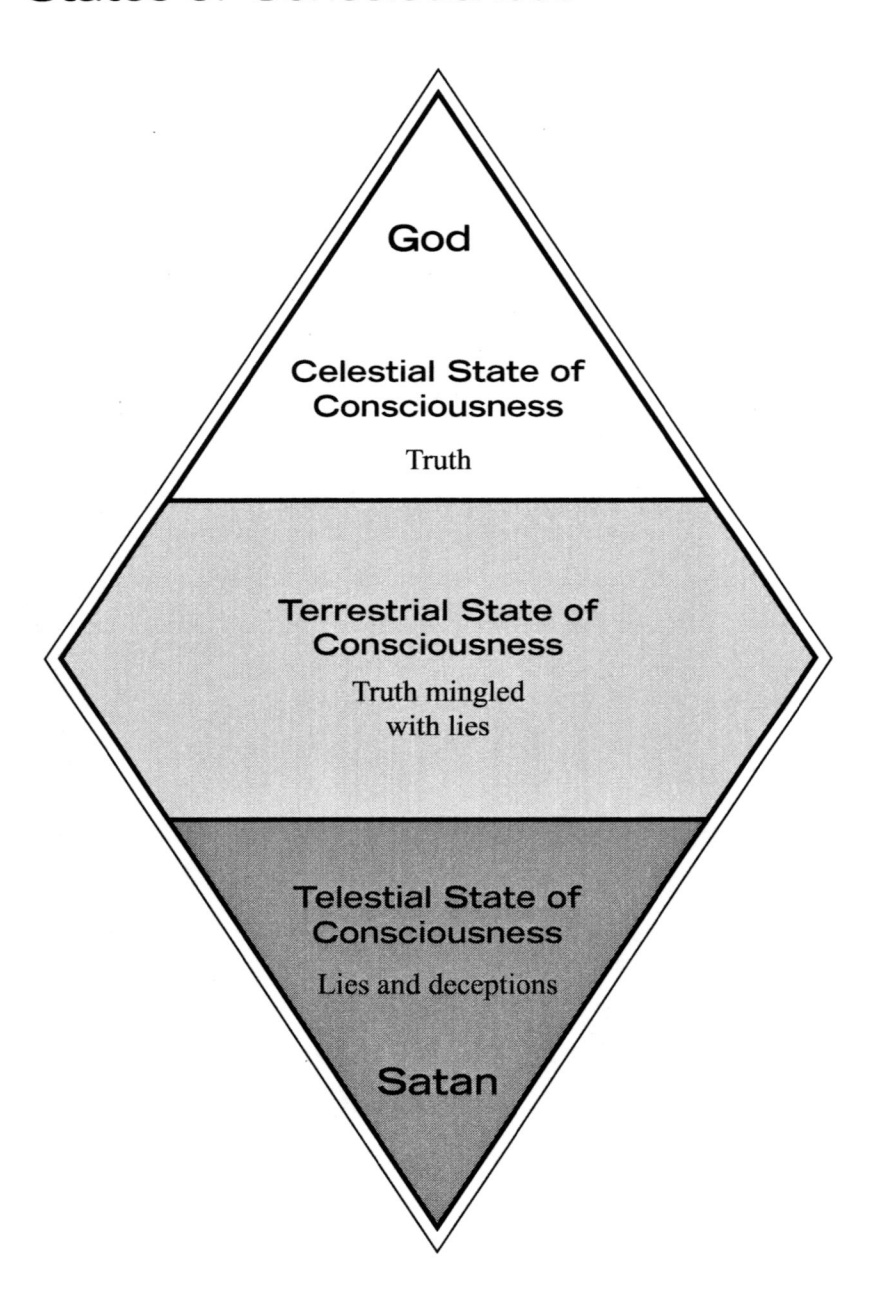

God

Celestial State of Consciousness

Truth

Terrestrial State of Consciousness

Truth mingled with lies

Telestial State of Consciousness

Lies and deceptions

Satan

CHAPTER 4
The Train from Shame to Recovery

....

The most important thing a person will do in this life is to learn how to think. Every thought and action generates the fuel that maps our journey on the "train to life" or the "train to nowhere". The price for a ticket on the train to nowhere is a lie. The cost of a ticket on the train to life is truth.

The train to life leads to peace, love, and serenity. The only way to board the train to life is to be in the spiritual mind, where God is the conductor. This means living an honest life no matter the cost.

IQ, EQ, AND SQ

On the train to life you have IQ, EQ, and SQ—mental

Thought Replacement Therapy

intelligence, emotional intelligence, and spiritual intelligence. When the switch, on the train to life is flipped, you can only

take IQ with you on the train to nowhere. Unfortunately, in this situation, your intelligence is significantly impaired because EQ and SQ cannot board the train with you.

Sometimes, despite our best intentions, we flip a switch, and our train becomes sidetracked. Circumstances in life have a way of derailing us and before we know it, we may be off on another track that leads to shame, blame, pain, and frequently, a terrible accident.

On the train to nowhere we are the conductors, thus, taking control away from God. As we cruise down the tracks of life, what are some of the circumstances that cause us to get sidetracked?

There are five major switches that take most of us off the train to life:

- Perceived injustices.
- Unresolved forgiveness issues.

- Looking back at what could or should have been.
- Fear.
- Negative childhood imprints or experiences.

All five of these unproductive thought processes flip a switch in our mind and we become the conductor on a train headed for a small or large train wreck. Our life is a sum total of numerous train wrecks which, if endured, can, and often do, bring us back to the train to life.

Conducting Our Children's Train

Sometimes we hop aboard our adult children's trains, wanting to be the conductor of their trains, too. This is not an uncommon scenario. Some parents, because of guilt, fear, or insecurity, feel they must support their son or daughter long past the time their child should be on his/her own. These parents end up enabling their children so they will not work or take responsibility for their own lives. Often the parents will mortgage their home, spend their life savings, and go into debt to support their children. Parents may take care of an adult child who has an alcohol or drug addiction problem, trying to rescue the child from a personal disaster—the natural consequences of self-destructive behavior. It is as if the child's train is soldered to the parents' train and the longer it remains connected the less likely the child will be able to become the conductor of his or her own train.

Unresolved Forgiveness Issues

A grandmother, Sarah, rescued her grandson, Tyson, who had sexually abused a neighbor girl. She hired an attorney, and moved him out of state so he would avoid charges. She couldn't bear seeing him suffer the consequences of his actions. Later, Tyson wrecked his car, and she financed a new automobile for him. Recently, Tyson moved in with her and her husband. He doesn't work or go to school. Sarah feels guilty about the way she raised Tyson's father and now feels obligated to compensate—trying to rectify her former mistakes by taking care of Tyson's every need. She will say and do whatever it takes to keep him out of trouble.

Tyson's grandmother doesn't want to see him suffer and wants to rescue him from natural consequences. She is trying to become Tyson's savior. In reality, she is not allowing Tyson to learn and grow from the choices he makes.

Sarah's husband, Bill, is not in agreement with her decision regarding her desire to rescue Tyson. Sarah's marriage as well as their retirement is in jeopardy. Sarah accuses Bill of not supporting Tyson and passes blame onto Bill for the way he raised their son. This makes Bill feel like he is being held hostage to his wife's decision to mortgage their home and spend their life savings to save their grandson. Symbolically, Sarah is trying to fix Tyson's train every time it breaks down, keeping him on the train to nowhere for a longer period of time. At the same time through lack of forgiveness, for herself and Bill, she is believing the ultimate lie that she can save Tyson. Tyson, is not learning or growing from his mistakes by accepting responsibility for his actions. Instead, he has learned that his grandmother is willing to accept the consequences for his actions.

Keeping the Marriage on the Right Track

When a couple marries, they can either ride on a train together, with God as the conductor, or they can ride on a train together with the dominant person conducting the train. If the conductor has poor eyesight, or a dimly lit filter of the mind, both parties will head down the wrong track, straight toward a major train wreck.

Perhaps, you are the passenger at times and the conductor at others. In some marriages, it may even be possible for both people to be on different trains. One person may be on the train to life and freedom, with God as the conductor, and the other on the train to nowhere. In such cases, it is painfully difficult to stand by and watch a train headed for a wreck.

Other times, individuals see a train headed for nowhere, but want to board the train anyway and ride along with the misguided conductor.

Brett and Helen

Helen jumped on board a fast moving train to nowhere with Brett. Brett said all the right things—everything Helen wanted to hear. Rarely, though, was he honest with her. He promised to spend time with her, but he often broke his word, rationalizing away the seriousness of the situations with lies. When caught, he always had an excuse.

Eventually, it was revealed that Brett had lied to many people during his young life. He lied to his friends, Helen's mother, and many others. However, Brett reassured Helen that he would never lie to her!

Once Helen's mother asked Brett what kind of grades he received. Brett proudly announced, "Mostly 'F's,' but sometimes I'm lucky and earn 'D's."

While Helen was in chemistry shock, her mother was in red flag shock. She continued to explain to Helen that Brett would surely become a "D" or an "F" provider, husband, father, and spiritual companion; he was bad news with all those red flags. How could Helen not see it?

Blindly, Helen fell in love with Brett and married him. Predictably, after they had their first child, Brett informed her that he did not love her anymore and, soon thereafter, left the marriage.

Usually family and friends, viewing things more objectively, try to convince their loved ones not to marry this type of person.

Helen was under the false impression that she could turn Brett around, or, better yet, love Brett so much that he would have a desire to do something with his life. However, Brett's train had so much momentum going in the wrong direction that Helen had little chance of stopping it and getting him to reverse the direction.

Inviting a Therapist on Board

As a therapist, I am invited to board other people's trains. I have boarded many trains, over 30,000 hours of trains. Initially, they show me around, where I can get a feel for the train right away. I am immediately able to detect the trains that are off track, which have learned to travel that way most of their lives. Other trains are dismantled and temporarily out of commission. Sometimes all they need is a part replaced, or perhaps an overhaul to get started again. Sometimes the only problem is a change of oil or a higher grade of fuel to keep the train running smoothly.

I consider it a privilege that someone would let me view his or her train from the inside. I see so many trains passing by during the day, but I can take this special time to board their train. Let me take you on such a journey and tell you what I see.

On most trains, pictures of early memories and significant events, as well as losses, line the walls. The losses seem to direct the heart of the train. This is always a sacred room, and I am aware of the meaning when a person shows me this room. This is a "where were you" room. Where were you the day Kennedy was killed? Where were you on 9/11? Where were you the day your brother came to your office and told you your father had hanged himself? Do you remember the sights? The sounds?

Where were you the day a patrol officer came to your door and told you your husband would not be coming home? Where were you the day you learned your son or daughter had been abused? Where were you the day you learned your parents were getting a divorce? Where were you the day you found out your husband or wife was having an affair? Where were you the day you figured out there was no Santa Claus?

Yes, this room is big, and every event has a story—including all the days that led up to the event and the days shortly after. And, yes, these losses affect the way your train operates.

There are also smaller, but still very significant, losses. Where were you the day you told someone the truth about your life, and they rejected you? How did that make you feel? Where were you the second time you told someone the truth about your life and they, too, rejected you? Is it two strikes and you're out, or three strikes and you're out?

Sometimes I board a family train, where everyone is being held hostage with tape over their mouths. The secret of violence or some other horrific tragedy clouds the recovery of this family. Immediately, I am aware that many of the people will not survive well in this life. Some will have anxiety disorders, and others will have explosive disorders. But the people are resilient. This train is a little hard to board, because the fate of the passengers is questionable at best. To me, this looks like a train that is going to war every day, and at the end of the day, many of the survivors of the train will have Post Traumatic Stress Disorder. Some will want to jump to their death—anything to get off the train to nowhere. However, they are being held hostage, and not much can be done, even with protective service. On occasion, a prisoner of war will escape the holocaust, but at a very high cost. The only escape for a member of this train is the "spiritual train." This person will gladly give up their right to drive their own train for the Savior's train. They will be nurtured, fed, and cared for on the train to life.

Sometimes I board a child's train and I know they want unconditional acceptance. They want what everyone wants—to be heard and understood. They want someone to care about what they are thinking and feeling. They are so innocent and trusting that they are fine with anyone who wants to be the conductor.

Sometimes people bring other people aboard their train to help them heal. This is good, but once the passengers are ready to board their own trains, they need to be released with love. People need to feel like they can board another train without ever being held hostage—either by the passengers or the conductors.

Many times people come to my office after a small or serious "train accident." Sometimes they are filled with shame and wish they had been more cautious, or that the accident had never occurred.

Jim's Story

Jim buried all of his train wrecks under lies. He minimized and rationalized every experience. Once Jim wanted the family to move to another home, so he set the house on fire. He never admitted that he did it on purpose. The whole incident was buried alive with lies. Jim also viewed pornography on the family computer, but denied that he had ever used the computer for anything that would be considered inappropriate.

Jim told so many lies that he began to believe his own lies. The only way to get this train up and running was to resurrect each car that was buried under lies. Once the truth was exposed the healing could begin.

Family Train

When I board a family train, I get a feel for the passenger on the train and recognize who the conductor is. I get a passenger list as well as a history of previous passengers that have been on the train. I look at the course and destination of the train. I sometimes take a quick view of their maps. I look at their history. I ask myself if the train has a comfortable feel, or not. Does everyone onboard feel free to talk? Are the passengers safe? What are the things that derail the train? Is there any fear of other people on the train? Can everyone grow and become who they are? Do some family members have to walk on eggshells? What are the family secrets? Can the family members be okay if secrets are told, or will the shame be too great for them to overcome and survive?

In an enmeshed family, if someone makes a critical mistake, everyone feels like they made that mistake. This train is filled with shame and secrets. The only way to get that train up and running is to open the door and let all the secrets out. It may also be necessary to help everyone realize they are individuals, with their own free agency, and that people can make different choices in life.

Sometimes we board a train with our co-workers. This can be a pleasant or unpleasant experience, as the case may be. Sometimes we need to board another's train to take shelter from a storm in relationships in the workplace. It may be a scary experience as we depart the train of shelter, but ultimately, we will have to stand on our own.

We must stop driving other people's trains; they need the driving experience. They need to become self-reliant. We need to step off their train and lovingly surrender the train back to them. Pull the switch that says, "Stop the Train." Step back from the train and say, "Woo! Woo! Goodbye to the Chattanooga Choo Choo!"

We need to work at fixing our own train that was dismantled so long ago and board it again. We may have to release several cars so our trains can run more smoothly. It may require uncoupling cars that slow our trains down.

One train wreck I often have occurs when I fail to watch for stop, yield, or similar warning signs. I get my train going so fast that when I see these signs, I tend to keep on going anyway. During such times, I have to stop and take care of myself. Remember, it only takes one train wreck to change your life.

Find out what flips your switch onto another track of reality. Is it fear, pride, envy, lust, negative self-talk, greed, or the inability to forgive yourself or others? All of theses mindsets will take people off the train to life. Don't let lies be the fuel that runs your train, or you will have a horrific jolt as your train crashes into an unyielding wall.

Other cars that may need to be removed from your train might be the "divorce" car; the "I'll bury this car under lies" car; the "addiction" car, and, especially, the "I can't forgive myself/or others" car. And don't forget the "I care what other people think of me" car. Recognizing that these cars, if taken on, will delay or derail your targeted destination, is helpful.

Draw your own train in life. Put emotions on the cars and even relationships. Which cars do you need to let go of? Who is the conductor of your train? Which cars hold you back, and which cars help you move forward? We have relationships in life that

Thought Replacement Therapy

help us move forward, and others that hold us back. You know those individuals who support you and try to help you reach your goal to move your train forward. Identify those who are constantly trying to redirect your train.

Picture yourself releasing the car that holds you back. Maybe you can start your own salvage lot for those cars that you no longer need or want. If you need to, you can always go back and pick up the car that caused you so much pain. It will always be there, waiting for you. But just for now, release the car that holds you back, especially the fear car. Fear of what others will think, fear of failure, fear of success, etc...

Woo! Woo! You have boarded your own Chattanooga Choo Choo!

CHAPTER 5
How to Discern Healthy and Unhealthy Relationships

....

There are many addictions in this life, including alcohol, drugs, food, money, sex, shopping, etc. The list goes on and on. Addictions are often used to escape truth and feelings. But the addiction I am going to address is the unhealthy relationship addiction. Let's compare it with food because everything you do with food, you do with relationships. Likewise, everything you do with relationships, you do with food. If someone has a tendency to restrict healthy food they may have a tendency to restrict healthy relationships. If a person has a tendency to compulsively overeat food that is not good for them, they may also have a tendency to gravitate toward obsessive and unhealthy relationships.

To illustrate this concept, I will begin with an analogy, likening a grocery store to the story of Eve in the Garden of Eden. In the Garden of Eden, Satan encouraged Eve to partake of the forbidden fruit so she could *"...be as gods, knowing good and evil." (Genesis 3:5)* She chose to believe Satan because she wanted to be wise. She believed his lie, ate the fruit, and fell from the spiritual realm into the temporal realm. She confessed, *"The serpent beguiled me, and I did eat." (Genesis 3:13)*

Many foods are infused with chemicals and artificial coloring. Foods may be heavily processed and have little nutritional value. They may look and taste good to the temporal eye and palate but offer little or no sustenance.

Often, too much emphasis is placed on the packaging of the food, and too little on the food itself. In interpersonal relationships, there is a strong desire for instant gratification, especially if the "package" is physically attractive and alluring. When there is a strong chemistry between a man and woman, emotions may hamper the ability to think clearly or choose wisely. Similar to grocery shopping when hungry.

Hot Fudge Sundaes vs. Asparagus

One of the most important decisions we will make in this life is whom we will marry. There are two basic types of men and women you could fall in love with. One is the "hot fudge sundae" man or woman, and the other is the "asparagus" man or woman.

Unlike the asparagus partner, it seems you can never get enough of the hot fudge sundae partner. You find yourself staying awake through the night worrying about where that partner is, and what that partner is or is not doing. It's also very hard to stay away from the hot fudge sundae—it's so easy to come back to this type of partner time and time again, even though you know that the person is really not good for you. The hot fudge sundae partner always seems to know when you are the most vulnerable—that's when he or she calls, texts, or sends you an e-mail and breaks your resolve to rid yourself of this unhealthy habit. A hot fudge sundae partner takes, and takes, and takes, and depletes your energy and spirit. And, unfortunately, hot fudge sundaes are rarely around when you really need or crave them the most.

Hot fudge sundae people don't go that well with other people in your life. Others in your life may have a hard time with them—(mom and dad, friends, or your kids) and may even try to warn you about this person. Your hot fudge sundae friend will try and make you choose between your important relationships. It's not uncommon to have to enjoy them alone and the process is often fast! If you end up marrying a hot fudge sundae and have children with him or her, you'll probably pass on the craving for hot fudge sundaes to your posterity.

The Lord states, *"Be ye not unequally yoked together with unbelievers: for what fellowship hath righteousness with unrighteousness? And what communion hath light with darkness?"* *(II Corinthians 6:14)*

Let's take a good look at the characteristics of hot fudge sundae men or women. He or she may be any or all of the following:
- Are dishonest.
- Believe lies about themselves and others.

Thought Replacement Therapy

- Are undependable.
- Blame others.
- Manifest inconsistent behavior and thought patterns.
- Exercise poor judgment.
- Are selfish and take from others.
- Seek conquests.
- Hold grudges.
- Are often charismatic.
- Are hypnotic.
- On the surface, seem too good to be true.
- Use flattering words.
- Are superficial.
- Are control freaks.
- Believe the world revolves around them.
- May not get along with the rest of the family.

In addition, hot fudge sundae relationships have some of the following consequences:

- Loss of spirituality.
- Loss of family and friends.
- Loss of money.
- Weight gain or weight loss.
- Loss of opportunity for real love.
- Eventual loss of relationship.
- Living in a marriage prison.
- Loss of health.
- Loss of life.
- Watching children make poor choices.

- Multigenerational dysfunction.
- Total loss of self-identity.

These characteristics are not easily detected under their look-good, smell-good, taste-good embodiment. When someone falls in love with a "hot fudge sundae" man or woman, focusing on their exterior appearance, they miss the vital ingredients that keep a marriage together, which lie within the inner person, the heart and soul. Love that is based on temporal desires is usually a lie, and is more likely to end in sadness.

On the other hand, while the asparagus man or woman's appeal may not be as enticing or attractive as the hot fudge sundae, an asparagus partner truly has a longer shelf life and is a lot more reliable. The asparagus partner can be enjoyed by a broader range of people, (including your parents, your friends, your kids). They also give, and give, and give, and truly enhance your life. The asparagus-type partner is good for you. You never wake up in the middle of the night wondering what happened to him or her. You know he or she will still be in the house in the morning. In other words, the asparagus partner is faithful, loyal, reliable, and healthy.

The asparagus man or woman embraces characteristics found in those who are celestial minded. Asparagus men or women most often believe and embrace truth. They frequently give to enhance the lives of others.

Asparagus men and women are:
- Honest.

- Responsible.
- Inclined to exercise good judgment.
- Willing to sacrifice.
- Committed.
- Forgiving.
- Admired and respected by children and family.
- Salt of the earth.
- Honest about their imperfections.
- Meek, in that they possess controlled strength.

It isn't uncommon for individuals to choose partners who reflect their own weaknesses or strengths.

What Keeps People from Real Love

Whatever separates you from God also separates you from your partner in a relationship or marriage.

Often, whatever you don't accept or forgive in your family of origin, you become, marry, or pass on to the next generation.

In the Old Testament, Esau sold his soul for a mess of pottage. He wanted what he wanted, and wanted it *now*. Today, this idea is exemplified by those who "can't wait," "can't be alone," and become involved in relationships too fast; or by those who feel vulnerable, or are experiencing a vulnerable time in their lives.

I know plenty of people who are addicted to the beginning energy and excitement of a relationship. In contrast no one is addicted to the ending of a relationship. Single people often feel inadequate, unworthy, alone, and afraid. They can become easy targets for the intrigue and forbidden "please connect with me and make me whole" type of feelings associated with early romantic relationships.

The following summarizes reasons why people have trouble developing a relationship beyond the superficial excitement:
- Inability to make correct choices or commitments.
- Take the relationship to a level of intimacy beyond the level of commitment.
- Unreasonable or limited expectations.
- Inability to trust themselves or others.
- Failure to take time to work on their own issues.
- Lack of motivation.
- Lack of possibilities—real or perceived.
- Inability to forgive self or others.
- Inability to love self or others.
- Embrace fear instead of faith.
- Tend to see things not as they are, but as they want them to be.

Common Lies

There are many lies that people tell themselves that allow them to enter into dysfunctional relationships, or to stay in a relationship even after finally seeing their partner for who he or she really is.

These lies may include:
- If people really knew me, they wouldn't like me.
- Why try to find a better relationship? I'll never find anyone better.

- I don't deserve anyone better.
- This relationship is better than being alone for the rest of my life.
- I'll never marry him or her; we just hang out together.
- The only reason I'm staying with him or her is for the children.
- If I love him or her enough, I can change him or her.
- He or she will eventually grow up.
- If no one knows (the secret/lie within our relationship), it won't matter.
- You just don't know him or her like I do.
- If I ignore the problem, it will go away.
- Being lost in the "desert" for however long lies are believed or ignored.

These are just a few of the lies people tell themselves while in a dysfunctional relationship.

If you can step back a moment and face a truth you might see the relationship for what it really is. One sure way to tell if you are headed into an unhealthy relationship is if your head and heart don't match. If your head is telling you one thing and your heart another—beware! Take a good look to see if you are being pulled into a relationship that fits this rule. If you are, let your head do the talking and your feet do the walking. Pay attention to the waving red flags and blaring smoke alarms! Indulgence in unhealthy relationships produces guilt, self-hatred, remorse, a sense of emptiness, and shame.

To an extent, all of us, at times, move back and forth, and

from side to side between the asparagus and the hot fudge sundae type of relationship, depending on if we are in our spiritual or temporal mind. A relationship becomes dangerous to the degree or extent the characteristics of the other person are predominantly hot fudge. Real love encompasses sacrifice, commitment, and forgiveness. Unreal love fosters selfishness, conquest of others, and the holding of grudges—what you might call a "hot grudge sundae!"

There are three ways to come to know a person and their relationship style:
1. Associate with him or her in a group setting.
2. Continue working and planning other activities with him or her, which can reveal if he or she has a hot temper, whines or complains a lot, or has other traits of a hot fudge sundae.
3. Marry him or her and then it is too late. Definitely not recommended. It is better to take the time to really get to know a person beforehand.

To complicate things, the more someone gravitates toward a physical relationship without the necessary deep spiritual connection, the more the person distances himself or herself from real love and the satisfaction associated with a meaningful and truly intimate relationship. This habit makes true intimacy impossible. Those seeking the drama and excitement of physical intimacy and romantic love too soon, may never have the opportunity to comprehend or experience a fulfilling union with another. They experience the chemistry or attraction, and even addiction, to the physically exciting element, albeit unreal and unfulfilling.

While real love allows a person to be imperfect and allows others to make mistakes, real love is also reality-based. Unreal love can't stand to make mistakes or to be wrong. It covers up, glosses over, or does whatever it takes to force the relationship. Sometimes hot fudge sundae partners will claim to see only the good in others, refusing to acknowledge imperfections in themselves or others. People often become attracted to another's potential, not viewing them as they really are. They spin a story or lie viewing the individual through rose-colored glasses; or seeing them as they imagine they could be instead of who they really are. Denial is the operative word.

Your chances of finding lasting love improve when you foster and build a relationship in your spiritual mind. When someone falls in love with an "asparagus" man or woman they fall in love with their mind and heart or the inside person.

CHAPTER 6
Our Relationships Mirror Our Relationship with God

....

Often, our relationships with others are a mirror image of our relationship with God, in that whatever separates us from God also separates us in our relationships with others. Can you imagine the power of this concept? Let's take a look at some examples so we can understand it more fully.

Addicted to Another's Potential

A handsome, well-dressed young man named Mike walked into my office one day. He told me he grew up in a family where his father was, as he described, 50 percent religious and 50 percent spiritual. He described his mother as 100 percent religious. He differentiated "religious" as the knowledge of beliefs, and "spirituality" as living the knowledge of beliefs.

Mike related that his mother cared more about looking good and what other people thought than what God thought. He also described her as a manipulator who said and did whatever she needed to get her way.

At the age of sixteen, Mike stopped going to church. He drank on occasion and struggled with morality issues. In his later teens he dated Janis, a religious, conservative girl for whom he felt love. At the same time he was also having a sexual relationship with another woman for whom he felt lust. In actuality, he was doing a great job of fence sitting—living with one foot in the temporal world and the other in the spiritual.

His parents wanted him to go on a mission for their church, which was expected of young men his age, but each wanted him to go for a different reason. Both were concerned about how it would look to others if he didn't go; however, his father also had some genuine concern for his son's spiritual growth. They finally pressured him to go to their ecclesiastical leader, to whom Mike confessed his immoral behavior. Because Mike seemed penitent, the leader also encouraged him to serve a mission. Mike remembers feelings of overwhelming pressure to go, so he reluctantly relented.

During his mission, he remained in contact with Janis. After returning home, he found Janis living with another man. She explained that she had been date raped by this man, and ended up moving into his home, where she continued to have sex with him "against her will." It would be an understatement to suggest that Janis was in denial.

Despite all of this, Mike married Janis after dating for only a few months. The first year of their marriage was rocky. Mike said he was angry at God for "allowing" his girlfriend to be raped while he was on a mission. Needless to say, Janis' family background also contributed to the couple's inability to acknowledge reality.

Mike considered his mother-in-law's thought processes bizarre and confused, impacting many of her decisions. She used psychotropic medications to numb her emotional pain. Mike harbored concerns that his wife would turn out like her mother.

After being married for five years, Janis wanted a baby, but Mike felt a child would lock him into their relationship, and he was not ready to make that big of a commitment. Incidentally, Mike admitted that if he divorced, he would not continue going to church.

Is there a mirror image apparent? Was Mike born into a religiously active family? Yes. Was Mike a mirror image of his parents? Mike liked to look good, but ultimately, he said and did what he wanted. It's likely his parents said, "We did everything right, but still he fell away from the church." Mike mirrored this thought process when he believed he had done everything right by going on a mission, and his girlfriend had been raped. Both Mike and Janis broke their commitment to God and ultimately broke their commitment to each other.

Lack of Sincere Commitment

Richard was active in his religious congregation and held numerous positions. He was intelligent, charming, charismatic, and had a wonderful sense of humor. Over the years there was a consistent pattern that made his actions an interesting case study. He worked hard, however, he was constantly complaining and had a pattern of backing out of commitments with family, friends, and neighbors at the last minute—he always had an excuse. Let's look at how this pattern plays out as a mirror image with his daughter.

One of Richard's greatest trials was associated with his daughter who struggled with addictions. While Richard served God in a demanding church position, his daughter, Lisa, stopped using drugs and returned to church activity. Ironically and coincidentally, as Richard backed out of his church position, Lisa went back to using drugs and left the church. Could our children's behavior be a reflection of our relationship with God?

Didn't Want to Work

Chris was a man who had a difficult time keeping his commitments to his employer. He frequently found excuses not to go to work. Strangely enough, he was still employed after several years. During this same time, he was an active leader in his church. One day, he chose to resign from his church position. Soon afterwards, he was also fired from his job. While not all people lose their job because they neglect church service, in this instance, there seemed to be a connection. Could it be that his noncommitment behavioral pattern finally caught up with him, or did it have anything to do with his decision to break his commitment with God?

Lack of Forgiveness

Nancy was a woman who wanted her children to forgive and accept her. She had lived a rebellious life, and, on occasion, had been abusive to her children. However, she refused to forgive her parents, especially her mother, for similar treatment. And she continued to tell and retell her negative experiences to her children while they were growing up. Nancy went to numerous counselors, wanting them to work the miracle that only she could work by forgiving her parents. If Nancy had forgiven her parents, could she have been forgiven by her children, herself and God? Remember, you may pass onto the next generation whatever you don't accept or forgive in your family of origin.

Fear Wife Would Have an Affair

Russ started viewing pornography as a young teenager, at which time his first girlfriend left him for someone else. This devastated Russ and he was angry for many years. Over time, however, he had a change of heart and began to serve God by committing to go on a mission for his church. When he returned home, he met a wonderful young woman and they were married. The first ten years of their marriage they were both committed to God, but later

Russ returned to the world of pornography. Shortly after, his wife began an extra-marital relationship. Russ broke his commitment to God and his wife broke her commitment to him.

Eventually, Russ realized his family was being destroyed and committed to give up pornography for a designated period of time. Not coincidentally, at the end of this time, his wife confessed she was having an affair. He was able to forgive his wife for her infidelity and felt that God had forgiven him for using pornography; however, he remained concerned that his wife would not remain faithful. His counselor asked if he thought he would return to pornography again. He saw the correlation in this question and was determined to keep his own part of the bargain.

Fix My Son—He's Argumentative

One family was having problems with their son David, who was argumentative. They said that he constantly argued with his family and other siblings. Both parents had grown up in very religious families, but they had stopped attending church later on in life. They claimed to believe their faith was true, but they argued with God and other authority figures about everything. They felt they could be close to God without going to church. After all, they reasoned, most religious people are hypocrites.

Now their son was acting out and arguing with everyone. They wanted someone to intervene and "fix" their son. The family didn't see a need to change their relationship with God, only to change their son's relationship with them. The family refused to communicate with God, and felt quite upset that their children rarely communicated with them. When you stop loving and respecting God, is it possible that your children might stop loving and respecting you?

Commitment Leads to Happiness

When Danny came in for counseling, he was struggling with masturbation and pornography. Danny wanted to find a wife, but he couldn't give up "these pernicious habits." Over time, when he grasped this mirror image concept, he began to serve and love God the way he would want a spouse to serve and love him. He truly put God first. After a few years he met a wonderful woman who treated him the way he treated God. They both put God first, and their relationship thrived.

Lack of Will Power

Robert struggled with keeping commitments. Over and over he promised his wife, Sarah, that he would control his pornography addiction, but he always returned to it. Of course, Sarah soon lost her trust in Robert and their marriage was in jeopardy.

When Robert was asked if he would participate in church, he said he couldn't trust himself to commit to serving in a church position. Robert's inability to keep commitments was a common thread that ran through and affected every area of his life.

As Robert's spiritual filter became dimmer and dimmer he was led astray by his natural man mind. Robert no longer loved himself and became increasingly unable to love or respect anyone else. Robert's inability to make and keep commitments separated him from God, friends, his job, and ultimately his family.

Whatever separates people from God also separates them in their other relationships. Likewise, whatever separates people from loving God, keeps them from loving themselves, and whatever keeps people from loving themselves also separates them from loving other people.

Lost in the Desert

The story of Susan is like the Israelites who wandered in the desert for 40 years. Susan's actions were not in sync with her values and beliefs. One day she met John, who did not share her same spiritual beliefs. However, John said all the right things to Susan. In addition, he was a touchy-feely kind of guy who aroused emotions in Susan that had been dormant for many years. However, family and friends were not happy with her decision to date John.

One day, while walking through the church grounds, John promised Susan he would quit drinking and return to church. Susan agreed to marry John and tried to convince her family and friends that what John was telling her was really true—in spite of the fact that they believed otherwise. She became obsessed with changing John, but he actually changed her. He convinced her to break important spiritual commitments and to have a sexual relationship with him before they were married. They married, had a family, and, eleven years later, ended up in counseling.

John still drank and never did become active in church. John was frustrated that Susan didn't believe him—or in him; after all, he believed his own lies and needed her trust and support. John had numerous affairs, but he blamed Susan because she constantly nagged him.

Is there a mirror image here? Susan was unfaithful with her commitments and married someone who had not kept his commitments to her. The lies she believed created a distorted reality. The effect all of this has had on their children is a chapter in and of itself. Unfortunately, people are usually lost in the desert for the same number of years they choose to believe the lies that keep them wandering.

Fear of Loneliness

Barbara was a lovely woman who grew up in a religious family. Somewhere along the way she veered off the spiritual path. She had a tendency to put men before God, and the men she dated had a tendency to put other women, alcohol, and money before her. She had been divorced several times.

Then Barbara became involved with a man who had many attributes she was looking for in a spouse; however, he wanted to be with her only when it was convenient for him. Understandably, Barbara didn't feel cherished. Coincidently, she frequently found it difficult to get up at 9:00 a.m. to attend her church meetings, and it was not uncommon for her to refuse church service when it wasn't convenient. Does she love God and cherish her relationship with Him or, does she make a connection with God only when it is convenient?

Unresolved Anger

Jack's father had a pornography addiction and left his mother for another woman. Jack's mother became bitter with the church and blamed the leaders for not fellowshipping her husband into activity. Jack grew up and married Jill, who was active in her church affiliation. Jack carried his mother's attitude and he too couldn't forgive the church leaders and attended church begrudgingly. Later this couple ended up in counseling because Jack's wife couldn't forgive him and admitted that she stayed in the marriage begrudgingly.

To Be Forgiven You Need to Forgive

Imagine that someone called you everyday for three months to tell you they were going to paint your house and put on a new roof, but then, never came. How would that make you feel? Do we ever do that to God? Do we say we are going to pray, read the scriptures, or give up some pernicious addiction such as pornography, but we don't.

Every time I am tempted to get mad at someone, I have to ask myself if I have ever done that to God and 99.9 percent of the time the answer is yes. When we choose to break our commitment to God we need to be prepared to have someone else break their commitment to us. And then when someone breaks their commitment to us, and we forgive them, we are truly being forgiven by God as well as forgiving ourselves. If this works in a negative way it would also stand to reason that it would work in a positive way. Think about how that could work. Is it true that when people impart wisdom they also receive wisdom? When we truly forgive others we will also be forgiven by others. When we serve others, we will also notice blessings from God. Is this like Godhood 101 or is it a graduate course for this life as we progress into the next?

Return to Church

The instructor of a seminar explained he had worked with Lisa and Sam who had separated for a number of years. During the time they were separated they had not been intimate. He said that in only three months of therapy they were back together and intimate for the first time in many years. Almost as an afterthought, he said something very interesting. He said, "Incidentally, at the same time they began therapy, they also began to return to church activity after spending a number of years being inactive because one of them had been upset with God." Of course, I immediately saw the correlation between the couple coming closer to God and coming closer to each other.

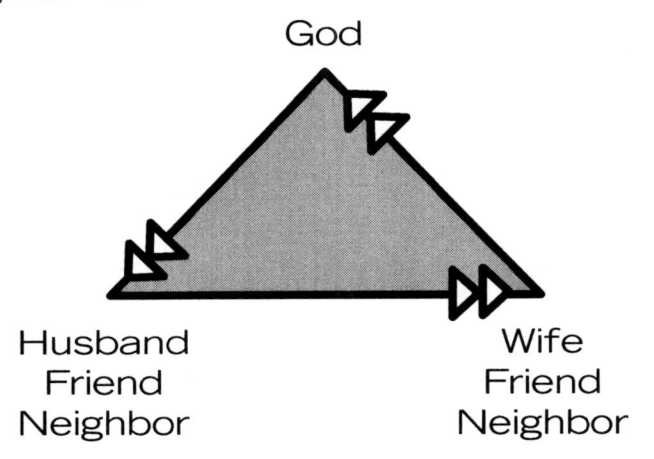

```
                    God
                     △
                    ╱ ╲
                   ╱   ╲
                  ╱     ╲
                 ╱       ╲
                ╱_____╲
         Husband            Wife
         Friend             Friend
         Neighbor           Neighbor
```

The closer relationships come to God, the closer they come to each other. I believe this is true not only in this life, but also for those who have gone before us.

People often want temporal blessings but are unwilling to sacrifice spiritually. However, not all failed relationships can be blamed on a partner's lack of effort to draw closer to God. Sometimes a disconnect within a relationship can occur when one party moves into a higher level of spiritual consciousness as the other remains, or even degenerates into a lower level of spiritual consciousness. Often the dissonance becomes too great for the relationship to survive in a healthy state. Therefore, relationships that are formed in the celestial and terrestrial state of consciousness have a much better chance of surviving.

Watch how a partner treats God, because that is how he or she will ultimately treat you. The way you relate to God is the way you will relate to all other relationships.

Do Our Relationships Mirror our Relationships with God?

The following worksheet is designed to help identify how your relationships mirror your relationship with God and others. Since all temporal problems have spiritual solutions, often by analyzing and identifying the spiritual problem (such as a dishonest relationship with God) we can resolve many relational and life problems. Improving our relationship with God improves all other relationships. This truth—like all truth—will set you free.

Our Relationships Mirror our Relationship with God

Complete the following:
1. I feel forsaken by _____ because _____. (Have we ever forsaken God or others?)
2. I can't forgive _____ because _____. (Is there anything we need to be forgiven for? Do we ever reject our self or God?)
3. One thing that makes me angry is _____. (Is there anything we are trying to control or are unwilling to surrender?)
4. _____ always breaks his or her commitments to me. (Do we ever break our commitments to God or others?)
5. _____ is only there for me when it is convenient. (Are we around for God and others only when it is convenient?)
6. _____ always/sometimes lies to me. (Do we ever lie to God, our self, or others?)
7. _____ only calls or comes around when he or she needs or wants something. (Do we pray or try to communicate with God only when we need or want something?)

CHAPTER 7
Is There No Other Way?

....

Throughout each day, we make choices, from what we choose to eat for breakfast in the morning, to what we choose to read, with whom we spend our time, to what we watch on television, and, finally, what time we turn out the light at night. From one moment to another, we continually find it necessary to make one decision after another. Many of these choices provide grand opportunities to learn the difference between truth and lies and discern between good and evil.

Let's draw an analogy that the whole earth is like the Garden of Eden. Eve was given a commandment not to partake of the forbidden fruit. When she broke the commandment and partook of the fruit, her eyes were opened and she was able to discern good from evil, and truth from lies. Could this be one purpose of our mortal experience? How many "forbidden fruit" experiences occur in our own lives? Have you ever made a choice that caused you great pain?

Much like Adam and Eve in the Garden of Eden, forbidden fruits entice each of us every day. These come in a variety of forms, including relationships, food, alcohol, drugs, pornography, and many others. Who do you choose to be with? Is your spouse someone you can trust? Is he or she someone God can trust? Do you put God first, or are you tempted instead to put first the counterfeit satisfactions of unhealthy food or unreal love? How do you spend your time?

When we partake of the forbidden fruit, it becomes part of us. Whatever separates us from truth and God separates us from recovery and binds us to addictions and other temporal thoughts and actions. When people bite into the forbidden fruit, they build a wall of lies to cover the shame, which causes even more pain and suffering. The only way to become "unstuck" or detached from the lies and other forbidden fruit is by attaching oneself to God and moving into a celestial state of consciousness. This is true even if the lie is about feelings.

Like Adam and Eve, we may also be tempted to run and hide after making a mistake. Perhaps a woman chooses a husband who betrays her by having an affair or by becoming addicted to pornography. She may choose to cover up the transgression by telling herself that it never occurred, or that it's not that big of a deal. Both of these responses are a type of lie. She may even lie and blame herself by thinking that if she were thinner or prettier her husband wouldn't have strayed. She may tell herself that if she forgives him or trusts him he will make the same mistake again—more lies. A more likely scenario is that he will not be able to forgive or love himself and will tell her that he no longer loves her when, in reality, he no longer loves or respects himself.

No one said this earth life was going to be easy. Learning to make right choices is one of the main purposes for this life. Making choices and learning from their consequences is the only way we can learn to discern truth from lies.

One way to help a spouse, family member, or friend become more comfortable about revealing their secrets or lies, to become more honest and open, is to be more loving and forgiving. You can encourage others to move into their spiritual mind or celestial state of consciousness by your reaction to their truth. Forbidden fruit experiences can present us with the opportunity to make a conscious choice to reside in a higher state of consciousness.

Reaping Rewards from Good and Bad Choices

In the New Testament, Satan tempted Jesus after Jesus had fasted for forty days and forty nights. Satan used the three primary temptations of the flesh: appetites, wealth, and power. Jesus faced the temptation of appetites because He hungered for food. He faced the temptation of wealth, when from the height of a mountain, the riches of the world were said to be even greater than the vistas before Him. He faced the temptation of power when from the pinnacle of the temple the power over legions of angels was offered to Him.

However, Satan failed in his attempt to get Jesus to accept the temporal and counterfeit forms of what only God can truly give. Satan can offer only a counterfeit—the temporal—which eventually brings more sorrow and suffering and is not lasting. In contrast, God promises and delivers joy beyond the temporal. He promises His gift of all that He has, and all the true power and glory that accompany it.

As Satan tried to tempt Jesus during His physically weakest moments, we too will be tempted and tried by the things of this world—lust, power, pride, money, and even unhealthy relationships. Often we are tempted when we are in a weakened and vulnerable state.

From the moment we open our eyes each morning, choices bombard us—choices between good and better, choices between better and best, choices between good and bad, and other choices between bad and worse. Myriads of carnal pursuits will tempt us. During our physically and spiritually weakest moments, we will be tried by the temptations of this world. We are all enticed daily to pursue and partake of worldly pleasures, often by peers who may encourage us to set aside our values and beliefs.

Rising Above Suffering

While suffering often occurs as a result of the poor choices we make, it can also come through no fault of our own. Loss will be a part of our mortal experience; no one is exempt from the trials of this temporal experience.

Even though our losses may weaken us, over time, we can rise again. We may grieve for our losses, and through the grieving process, we are saying, in essence, "Let this cup pass," which is a healthy response. None of us like grief in our lives and would prefer to have it pass us by. Our critical decision is how we respond to this grief. Losses either bring us closer to God or distance us from Him—depending on how we choose to respond. If we choose to attach ourselves to God, we begin to detach from the pain and sorrow. The key is in how well we are able to accept, forgive, surrender, and move forward after incurring a loss.

Entering Another's Garden

You can give someone a true gift if you enter their Gethsemane and *walk beside* them in their pain and suffering. If they can trust you enough to expose their wound to you and can feel totally accepted by you in spite of their wound, their healing and spiritual growth begins.

However, never walk in another's garden unless you are invited. One reason people will not allow others in their garden is because of the fear of rejection. If invited, walk beside them and, if allowed, view their wound in life. Don't try to take their wound away. The wound was most likely inflicted in childhood and reinforced in their adult life. The sins of the fathers are truly visited on the heads of the children. Wounds are passed down from one generation to the next for a purpose. Try to love the person, unconditionally, in spite of the wound. Then gently and lovingly pray for and with them.

You may be tempted to weed and beautify someone's garden

when they are not present. If you have a tendency to do this, picture a padlock on their garden gate. Even if someone wants to turn the key to their garden over to you, don't take it. If they leave cleaning and weeding instructions, they are turning their power over to someone who is willing to wrongly assume responsibility for their life.

At the end of our earthly experience we will all have something like a painting of our lives on a canvas. This picture will show that all the gardens have peaks and valleys, as well as, all the emotions such as fear, love, and sorrow, to name a few. If you could succeed in taking away the pain and sorrow of others, you may cause a white-out on their canvas of life.

Children need to have forbidden fruit experiences so their eyes can be opened and they can know good from evil. If you are an enabler, the white-outs you cause in others' lives could end up as a collage of enabling on your canvas. At the end of your life, your life picture could be made up of other peoples' lives. Often, trying to overcome for others is a distraction so you don't have to see the unpleasant details in your own picture of life.

One way to step away from another person's garden is by saying "No," or setting boundaries and lovingly accepting others as they are. Perhaps you can see their weeds and flowers, but you need to accept the fact that, ultimately, they have to do their own gardening.

CHAPTER 8
The Gethsemane Map

....

As our exemplar and advocate with the Father, the Savior has provided a map for us to follow as we experience our own personal Gethsemanes. I call it *"The Gethsemane Map."*

"I am crucified with Christ: nevertheless I live; yet not I, but Christ liveth in me: and the life which I now live in the flesh I live by the faith of the Son of God, who loved me, and gave himself for me." (Galatians 2:20)

A modern-day Gethsemane may include the following experiences and characters that played a distinctive role in the life of Christ prior to His crucifixion.

One: Our Gethsemane—Recognition of Personal Loss

Recognizing the imminent suffering and death He was about to encounter, Christ asked, while in the Garden of Gethsemane, that the bitter cup be removed. Nevertheless, He submitted His will to the Father's. Often, we are faced with a personal Gethsemane.

A modern-day Gethsemane could include the loss of a marriage or another valued relationship, death of a loved one, abuse, or loss of money, job, self-esteem, health, etc.

All of us, at times, will pass through what I call: The Eye of the Gethsemane Needle and, as we do, we will hopefully emerge with greater character and greater understanding of the true meaning of this earth life experience.

Two: The Judas-Mind—Betrayal

In the New Testament, Judas, one of Jesus' apostles, went to the Romans and asked how much they would pay him to identify Jesus. With a kiss on the cheek, Judas betrayed his friend for "thirty pieces of silver." Our Gethsemanes are sometimes caused by betrayal of one we consider a dear friend, loyal work associate, a colleague, or even a spouse, or grown child. It is even possible to betray ourselves.

When we tell a lie, break commitments or commandments, we open ourselves up to believing lies. Without the guidance of the Holy Spirit, we can sell our soul for a mere thirty pieces of silver without thinking of the long-term consequences. When we end up listening to the wrong voice, life presents a number of major consequences.

In Judas' spiritual mind, he loved Jesus; he was his disciple. But in his natural man mind, he betrayed Christ for thirty pieces of silver.

"And ye shall be betrayed both by parents, and brethren, and kinsfolks, and friends: and some of you shall they cause to be put to death." (Luke 21:16)

Three: The Peter-Mind—Fear and Co-dependency

Just after Jesus was arrested by the Roman soldiers, Peter, having been a loyal follower of Jesus, denied Jesus three times because of the fear of man. Peter also had an erroneous perception that he needed to shield Jesus from pain and suffering in this life. Do we ever give up who we really are because of our fear of what others might think? Do we try to be who others want us to be because of fear of rejection, persecution, or humiliation? Do we compromise our personal integrity by saying things that are not true? Do we also try to protect others from the pain and suffering in their lives?

In Peter's spiritual mind, he was a faithful follower of Christ. But in his natural man mind, Peter denied knowing Christ because of fear—fear of his life and of social rejection by association. It was also Peter's spiritual mind that allowed him to walk on water, and his natural man mind that no longer supported him in his effort to cross atop the Sea of Galilee.

Four: The Pontius Pilate-mind—To Be Seen of Men

In his position of prominence and power, Pontius Pilate was caught up in all of the entrapments found in today's modern society. His actions towards Jesus were not responsible. There was no reliable evidence against Jesus. However, Pilate's motivation was to give the crowd what they wanted. His desire for acceptance and admiration was "to be seen of men" because he sought approval from the outside world.

Pontius Pilate did not understand, nor did he agree with, the voices that wanted to crucify Jesus, but he did nothing to counteract the popular opinion.

When we encounter the downtrodden, or see others treated unfairly—do we stand up for them or not? Caring too much about popular opinion and how we might be viewed by others, do we let injustices slide by, or do we even become a party to these injustices?

In Pontius Pilate's spiritual mind, he understood that Christ was innocent; in his natural man mind, he was willing to placate the Pharisees and Sadducees to retain his status.

Five: The Mind of the Masses— Unrighteous Judgment

The masses ridiculed and condemned Jesus for declaring that He was the Son of God. They refused to accept truth. Instead, they asked Pilate to release Barabbas, a murderer, and crucify Jesus.

Do we live in a generation where those around us are choosing unrighteous values over more traditional moral values of right and wrong? What voices do we listen to? How do we judge ourselves and other people?

The Mind of the Masses represents the unrighteous voices that were raised against the Savior. Sadly, we have no account of knowing who would be in the spiritual and natural man mind amidst the rabble and clamor. Sometimes, caught up amid the din and tumult, it is difficult to distinguish between the spiritual and natural man mind.

Among the raucous crowd were the Pharisees and Sadducees shouting to save Barabbas and crucify the Savior. The Pharisees and Sadducees were two religious bodies at the time of Christ that believed in God and had the scriptures, but did not understand them or they would have recognized Christ for who he said he was, the Son of God. Thus, because of their lack of understanding and differing views, they competed with each other. The Pharisees esteemed themselves as perfect, putting themselves above others in self-righteous judgment. While the Sadducees mocked the idea of a resurrection. One way to remember the Pharisees and Sadducees is the Pharisees saw themselves as "fair-you-see," while the Sadducees were "sad-you-see." Perhaps at times in our own life, we take the role of a "fair-you-see" or a "sad-you-see."

Six: Crucifixion, Rejection, and Humiliation

Christ suffered at the hands of those He came on earth to save.

Have you ever made personal sacrifices for others, only to be humiliated, scorned, or rejected?

Christ has promised, *"Blessed are ye, when men shall revile you, and persecute you, and shall say all manner of evil against you falsely for my sake. Rejoice, and be exceeding glad: for great is your reward in heaven: for so persecuted they the prophets which were before you." (Matthew 5:11-12)*

Seven: Forsaken and Abandoned

Still, after doing everything right that you possibly can, have you ever felt deserted or forsaken by God? Do you feel abandoned, and that your prayers are not being answered? Do you feel that you are left alone in the world? With His friends at His side, Christ made His way to the Garden of Gethsemane. There He asked His beloved Peter, James, and John to stand watch during what would become His greatest trial. During the depths of His greatest pain, He returned to His friends and found them sleeping.

During our greatest pain, we, too, may find ourselves alone— bereft of the support of friends, or even family and loved ones. Too often, we do not recognize, or we refuse to acknowledge, that our only true watchmen during our greatest personal trials are God, our Eternal Father, and our Brother, Jesus Christ, who literally felt *everyone's* personal pain and anguish. They, alone, know the extent of our suffering and are the only ones who can truly give us succor, the only ones who can fully understand what we are experiencing. Christ also experienced desertion at the hands of those who called themselves disciples and friends at the very apex of His pain and suffering.

It is true that, at times, our mortal watchmen (parents, guardians, friends, etc.) fall asleep—often through ignorance or because of weaknesses such as addictions. Sometimes our watchmen are distracted by the daily efforts of trying to cope in this mortal sphere. Addictions, depression, self-deception, irresponsibility, neglect, preoccupation and the entire gamut of human frailties may also contribute to circumstances that make a caregiver less than adequate at one time or another.

"For a small moment have I forsaken thee: but with great mercies will I gather thee." (Isaiah 54:7)

"For the people shall dwell in Zion at Jerusalem: thou shalt weep no more: he will be very gracious unto thee at the voice of thy cry; when he shall hear it, he will answer thee. And though the Lord give you the bread of adversity, and the water of affliction, yet shall not thy teachers be removed into a corner any more, but thine eyes shall see thy teachers: And thine ears shall hear a word behind thee, saying, This is the way, walk ye in it, when ye turn to the right hand, and when ye turn to the left." (Isaiah 30:19-21)

Eight: Forgiveness—Freedom to Move On

Jesus said, *"Father, forgive them for they know not what they do." (Luke 23:34)*

Without forgiving others, we cannot progress from the natural man mind into the spiritual mind. Also, when we cannot forgive others, we become bound to our own pain and shame. It is only by forgiving others that we can truly be forgiven of our trespasses.

Often our darkest hour is before the dawn.

"To whom ye forgive any thing, I forgive also: for if I forgave anything, to whom I forgave it, for your sakes forgave I it in the person of Christ; Lest Satan should get an advantage of us: for we are not ignorant of his devices." (II Corinthians 2:10-11)

Nine: Surrender—Accepting God's Will

"Father, into thy hands I commend my spirit." (Luke 23:46)

We have two choices when the storm clouds of adversity mount over us. Like Christ, we can humbly plead for help or divine intervention. We can also recognize our trials as opportunities for spiritual growth.

Jesus surrendered His will and accepted the will of His Father. Can we surrender our will to God's will? Christ freely gave His life to complete His mission, thus laying down the natural man in submission to the spirit.

While it is definitely true that, as Christ said, *"My thoughts are not your thoughts, neither are your ways my ways" (Isaiah 55-8),* we are strongly admonished to throw off the natural man and gravitate toward the spiritual man.

Ten: Resurrection—Victory

After His spirit left His body, Christ moved to a higher spiritual sphere where He returned to His Heavenly Father—a process that all of us are asked to follow. Christ was able to let go of everything in this world and, after three days, rise again. He overcame the pain and suffering inflicted upon Him by others; He turned the worst trial into a complete victory.

After Jesus was crucified, He rose again—identified and sanctified by His wounds. In a similar way, many of us have childhood or adult wounds that are less visible. If these wounds are not healed, they can be transmitted to others. After traversing through the Eye of the Gethsemane Needle—wading through trials of rejection, humiliation, and crucifixion—we can find great comfort knowing we can be healed—that we can rise above these wounds. As we crucify our temporal desires, we resurrect our spiritual desires and become sanctified by our wounds. For every temporal loss, there is a spiritual gain.

Victory

The Gethsemane Map is a charted journey of necessary life experiences designed to increase our spirituality. It is a journey that carries us above the temporal thoughts where we become capable of living in the world but not of the world.

"If ye were of the world, the world would love his own: but because ye are not of the world, but I have chosen you out of the world, therefore the world hateth you." (John 15:19)

Jesus had a mortal mother and an immortal father. We, however, are born into a mortal family and inherit "natural man" qualities that are in opposition to God-like qualities. Thus, the natural man becomes an enemy to God unless he yields to the enticings of the Holy Spirit. When we first arrive into this worldly sphere, we depend upon our earthly parents—our watchmen—for all the basic needs to sustain life. It isn't until later in life that we, hopefully, become aware that we also have a Heavenly Father upon whom we depend for spiritual sustenance that we may overcome this temporal world.

Many of us will experience one or more childhood Gethsemanes, which, if overcome, will help us develop essential tools to overcome our adult Gethsemanes. *"For in much wisdom is much grief and he that increaseth knowledge increaseth sorrow." (Ecclesiastes 1:18)*

Renowned psychiatrist Scott Peck has stated that if your goal is to avoid pain and escape suffering, he would not advise you to seek higher levels of consciousness or spiritual evolution. It is not for others to save or fix you. Each individual is to save himself or herself by turning to God and repenting and keeping the commandments—this is the only path to truth and light.

Each individual must have his or her own life experiences, thereby learning to identify and choose that which is good over deceit and lies, and all that evil encompasses.

This is an eternal principle: You can only assist another person to whatever world of light and truth you have achieved. You cannot nurture another person emotionally, developmentally, or spiritually to a higher degree than that to which you have already achieved. It is a truism that one cannot lift another unless one is on higher ground.

The steps and emotions often experienced during a personal Gethsemane include the following:
- Recognition of a great loss
- Betrayal by someone else—or self-betrayal

- Need for outside approval
- Harsh or unfair judgment by others or yourself
- Emotional pain and suffering from feeling as if you are being crucified
- Feeling forsaken at times because you are convinced your prayers are not being answered

You can move through your Gethsemane experiences by:
- Changing denial to acknowledgement and, finally, acceptance
- Surrendering your will to God
- Forgiving others
- Evolving to a higher level of spiritual understanding and consciousness

"These things I have spoken unto you, that in me ye might have peace. In the world ye shall have tribulation: but be of good cheer; I have overcome the world. (John 16:33)

Thought Replacement Therapy

The Gethsemane Map

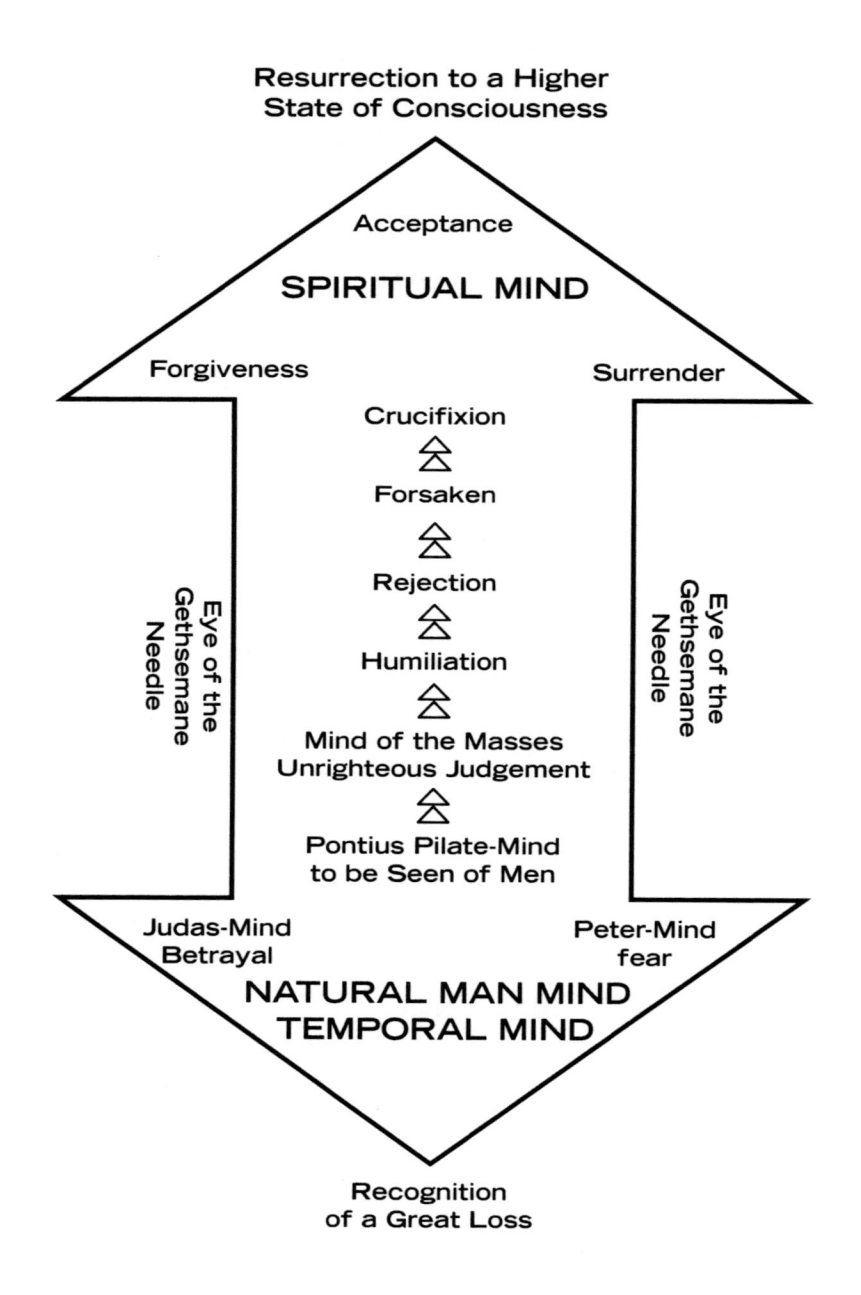

Resurrection to a Higher State of Consciousness

Acceptance

SPIRITUAL MIND

Forgiveness — Surrender

Crucifixion
△
Forsaken
△
Rejection
△
Humiliation
△
Mind of the Masses
Unrighteous Judgement
△
Pontius Pilate-Mind
to be Seen of Men

Eye of the Gethsemane Needle — Eye of the Gethsemane Needle

Judas-Mind
Betrayal

Peter-Mind
fear

NATURAL MAN MIND
TEMPORAL MIND

Recognition
of a Great Loss

CHAPTER 9
Recognition of a Loss

....

No one in this life is immune to the personal trials that, at some point or another, will crash against us, bringing us to the point of surrender and submission. Just when we think we can no longer endure another moment of pain and suffering, another wave brings us to our knees, and we question if we are capable of ever rising again. We may plead, "Please, Lord, take away this bitter cup." But if, in our darkest moments, we are able to cry out in complete submission, "Nonetheless, not my will, Lord, but Thine," He will give us the strength to rise to even greater heights, transformed and refined.

From the moment we are born, we begin experiencing our own temporal losses. As an infant, we may not get milk or comfort the second we cry for it. As a child, our first loss could be a toy or a piece of candy. Later, as a teenager, we may lose our first boyfriend or girlfriend; perhaps, we didn't receive the grade we felt we deserved, or didn't make the team, or lost some other long sought-after dream.

Later in life, we may lose a job, a fortune, a home, or even a spouse. At some point we will watch family members or friends die. We may also lose our physical abilities.

Four Stages of Loss

There are four stages of loss where a variety of experiences may occur. Let's look at these stages and the accompanying examples of possible loss. (Some losses may overlap between stages.)

Stage One—Childhood Loss

- Loss of will.
- Loss of being the center of attention.
- Loss of power.
- Loss of friends.
- Loss of pets.
- Loss of dignity and secure identity through humiliation or betrayal.
- Loss of a secure home (moving).
- Loss of siblings through marriage, drugs, mental illness, accidents, etc.
- Loss of parental security through parental depression, anxiety, health problems, mental illness, etc.
- Loss of security through betrayal at the hands of watch-

men—friends, parents, siblings, etc.
- Loss of security and safety through verbal, physical, emotional, or sexual abuse.
- Loss of loved ones through divorce or death.
- Loss of security through outside influences such as alcoholism, drug addiction, etc.
- Loss of physical, emotional, and/or mental health including developmental disorders, ADHD, learning disorders, autism, etc.
- Loss of physical or mental capacity.
- Loss of stability through change of school, friends, family, mother, father, pets, siblings, etc.
- Loss of spirituality.
- Loss of self-reliance.
- Loss of self-esteem through comparing self with others.
- Loss of control.

Stage Two—Teenage and Adolescent Losses

This stage includes the childhood losses, but adds several new experiences that often create new losses.
- Loss of first love.
- Loss of not being able to live up to one's own and others' expectations.
- Loss of positive image of self and others—sometimes by being belittled.
- Loss of realization that parents aren't perfect. They have problems.
- Loss of "Santa Claus" world when the realities of life emerge.

Thought Replacement Therapy

- Loss of security that comes from greater independence.
- Loss of virtue.
- Loss of spirituality.
- Loss of dependence on God.
- Loss of self-worth by rejection of others.
- Loss of trust, reputation, friends, family, etc. through betrayal of others.
- Loss through self-betrayal—accepting the lies told to self and others.

Stage Three—Adult Loss

- Loss of love.
- Loss of spouse or marriage.
- Loss of children.
- Loss of formerly obedient children through rebellion.
- Loss of money.
- Loss of career.
- Loss of educational opportunities.
- Loss of self-respect.
- Loss of health.
- Loss of job.
- Loss of parents.
- Loss of the ability to exert will on others.
- Loss of control.
- Loss of power (humiliation).
- Loss of acceptance (rejection).
- Loss of dignity through betrayal by friends, family, business associates, etc.

- Loss of aspirations and dreams.
- Loss of self-esteem through self-betrayal.
- Loss of trust.

Stage Four—Senior Losses

- Loss of spouse.
- Loss of financial security due to dishonesty, greed, deception, or betrayal by others.
- Loss of eyesight.
- Loss of hearing.
- Loss of memory.
- Loss of self-identity.
- Loss of friends.
- Loss of family and loved ones.
- Loss of the ability to make decisions.
- Loss of personal mobility.
- Loss of the ability to drive.
- Loss of the ability to care for self and others.
- Loss of independence resulting in increased dependence on family, friends, neighbors, etc.
- Loss of control.
- Loss of companionship.
- Loss of trust through humiliation.
- Loss of self-esteem or self-worth through rejection.
- Loss through betrayal by others.
- Loss through self-betrayal.
- Loss of life.

Lost in the Mail—Recognition of a Great Loss

Loss can be experienced in a myriad of ways.

Near the end of my mother's life, she was medically mismanaged and had a catastrophic medication reaction that resulted in her losing most of her cognitive abilities. Although her brain could barely function, she managed to express her great loss to me in a statement that haunts me to this day. She said to me, "Cynthia, I feel like I am 'lost in the mail.'"

Though my mother came into this world with nothing, she left this world a very rich person. She grew up in a family that worked hard to provide the necessities of life. Her favorite childhood story was about her desire to go to the fair with her friends. Her father, who was thrifty, gave her 25 cents to attend. However, she lost the quarter and he refused to give her another. She never forgot that experience and vowed to be more generous with her own family.

Another memory that shaped and framed her life was living through the Great Depression. She recalls her father going to the bank to withdraw all the family's money because he was afraid the bank would not withstand the depression. However, the bank president convinced him that his money was safe and told him that if he withdrew his funds, others might follow suit, creating a run on the bank. Her father decided to leave the money in the bank. During that era, if a bank failed or closed, there was no insurance on your money.

The next day, the bank closed and her father lost all of his money. A woman came into the house to change his sheets every half hour because they were soaked with perspiration from his mental turmoil. He lay in bed many days, suffering his own Gethsemane.

During this same period, my mother's sister, Naomi, died from rheumatic fever. My mother recalled her sister's death and how she was awakened in the middle of the night by a still, small voice that prompted her to go to her sister's side. It was that very night that her sister reached for my mother's hand to hold onto life and then silently and peacefully slipped to the other side.

These experiences, and others like them, shaped the course of my mother's life and mine, like the ripples in a pond, reaching down from one generation to another.

When I was sixteen years old, while driving my new automobile, the driver of another car ran a red light, injuring me and totaling my car. I was rushed to the hospital. That same day one of my mother's other sisters flew into town to see me. This aunt, who was like a second mother to me, was unable to take the stress of my accident, consequently, only hours after visiting me in the hospital, she died of a heart attack. This was a great loss for me and, for many years, I blamed myself for her death.

Yes, our family had everything money could buy, but still no peace. It appeared that we had so much that the world had to offer, yet we had so little spiritually; of God, we had nothing—or so it seemed. Only later, when I found a belief in God, did I find peace. And while life's trials did not end, my burdens have been lightened numerous times.

Do We Die the Way We Live?

I believe we die the way we live. As a child, I took Peter's role in our family. My self-proclaimed mission was to "save" my mother, but, unfortunately, her choices had devastating consequences. As a young child, I tried to help my mother make good decisions and continued to do so later in life. I seriously desired to protect her from all harm, but, of course, I never could.

Each person in a family takes on a different role. Sometimes, we are our parents' watchmen and sometimes they are ours. As my mother's health declined and she became more dependent upon me, I, like Peter, tried to save her from pain and suffering. I took her from one nursing home to another, trying to make sure she had the best care possible and that nothing bad would happen to her. I even sent people to stay with her during the day and spent most evenings with her after my work, but, in spite of my efforts, she was mis-medicated and lost 80 to 90 percent of her mental capacity. In a real sense, my mother died the way she had lived—with a multitude of losses.

I went through the grieving process hundreds of times. My grief was made more intense because I continued to take responsibility for not being able to save my mother from her final Gethsemane.

Peter passionately feared the arrest, persecution, and crucifixion he saw Jesus headed toward and tried in every way possible to protect and save Him. However, he learned that he could not take away another's Gethsemane, least of all, that of Jesus. Remember, the Gethsemane characters show up in your family of origin and in your work, church, clubs, neighbors, and all relationships.

When clients of mine bite into the "forbidden fruit," their

wounds are exposed and they feel shame and sorrow. At that moment, they want to unburden themselves with someone who is safe for them. Often, that is when they come into counseling, where they can go through the necessary and long overdue grieving process.

Recognition of the great loss can be devastating. These losses can involve the loss of self-esteem, self-worth, friendship, self-confidence, loss through betrayal or self-betrayal, and loss of relationship with family and God, to name a few. In situations like these, even the simplest thing may seem like a mountain too difficult to climb and be out of emotional reach, such as washing dishes or making a bed.

This path we tread is much like the path that Jesus trod. Whereas His greatest loss or trial ended in one day, ours may be extended over a lifetime. And each loss—or Gethsemane—prepares us for the next until the final day when our eyes meet His.

CHAPTER 10
"Let This Mind Be In You"

Let this mind be in you, which was also in Christ Jesus. (Philippians 2:5)

Our beliefs, good or bad, take us to many different worlds within our mind, perhaps worlds without number. These thoughts shape every aspect of our day-to-day lives and the direction of our future. Each of us is a creator in partnership with God or with the adversary. There is an author inside each of us. Even though we are the author, at times we may feel pain at the hands of others, or even at our own hands through the stories that we choose to listen to and adopt.

Julie's Story

Julie was born into a family that continually rewarded evil for good. Her father was more concerned with how the neighbors viewed the family than what his family thought of him. Her father's son, John, from a previous marriage, sexually abused her and several of her sisters. When the abuse was initially disclosed, the father seemed more defensive of his son's reputation than the well-being of the daughters who had been violated.

Julie thought her father never really liked her, and that she could never please him no matter what she did and no matter how perfect she became. Her stepbrother, John, was extremely rebellious, yet her father seemed to stand behind him no matter what he did. John was arrested for drugs and alcohol, dropped out of school, and caused the family a lot of grief because of his actions. Her father constantly made excuses and rationalized and minimized the seriousness of his son's rebellious behavior.

When Julie was growing up she didn't feel safe around her family because of the abuse and all the contention in the home. Her parents were verbally abusive and the family had no personal boundaries; consequently, Julie felt there was a complete invasion of her privacy. She didn't feel like she could stand up for herself because she was afraid of repercussions, therefore, she became more and more reclusive. Because she felt deeply betrayed by her family, everyone was perceived as a threat. The message she had received her entire life was that what she thought and felt didn't matter.

Eventually, Julie separated herself from her family. In her pain, she also separated herself from God and a spiritual connection.

Julie was worried about having a family of her own because she was afraid of passing on to the next generation her family's anger, guilt, and poor judgment.

Julie had sought therapy numerous times through the years, but nothing seemed to work; or, if it did, it wasn't lasting. She had completely neglected the spiritual part of her mind and heart and had built numerous walls to protect herself from the pain of the world.

She showed up in my office and wanted to know how to change a lifetime of fear and negative thinking. I told her it was impossible, unless she could come to understand the AM/FM concept. We talked about her spiritual mind and her temporal mind. I asked her to think about how she could recapture her mind from the AM station and move into the spiritual mind, the FM station. I also asked her to make a list of all the people who had betrayed her, including self-betrayal.

She needed to come to terms with the people she had not been able to forgive. Next, she needed to discover what was keeping her tuned to the AM station and what separated her from God and others, including her family. In her case, it was the fear of what people could do to her, as well as holding onto resentment towards herself and others.

In her childhood, Julie's watchmen had "fallen asleep." Even she had fallen asleep to the guidance and help of her internal watchman (Holy Spirit). She had, indeed, fallen asleep to the truth and had awakened to lies. For instance, she would spin a story to justify staying away from God and away from other people. We worked together to see how she could move out of her fear mind and into her spiritual mind. In other words, how could she remove the roadblocks and cross the bridge from the fear mind to her spiritual mind?

The number one reason people cannot enter into the sacred place of their mind is their inability to forgive self and others. Forgiveness and complete surrender is the price of this ticket. Remember, the higher the price, the greater the peace and insight. This means, the more you are willing to forgive, more will be given to you in the heaven portion of your mind.

The second greatest handicap to entering the spiritual mind is the tendency to believe lies. The only way to overcome this is to be completely honest with yourself and others. Sometimes disclosing the worst thing about yourself and recognizing you can still be forgiven and accepted is a very healing experience. Perhaps there is a secret you have never unlocked because of how painful it is. In spite of possible rejection and humiliation, maybe there is something you need to face or verbalize in order to begin the internal forgiveness process.

In order for Julie to heal, she needed to say "No" to her family and set firm boundaries instead of fearing rejection when she was open and honest with them. She needed to shift into her spiritual mind and become dependent upon God for her self-esteem. She was letting people who live in a telestial or terrestrial state of mind dictate who she was instead of letting God tell her who she was.

"Peace I leave with you, my peace I give unto you: not as the world giveth, give I unto you. Let not your heart be troubled, neither let it be afraid." (John 14:27)

Julie finally sought the peace she had allowed herself to be robbed of for so many years. Life had dealt her many blows and had contributed to so much pain in her life, but when she was willing to do whatever it took to surrender her will, she was able to move back into her spiritual mind. She became active in church, even though she had once promised herself that she would never return to a place where she felt so harshly judged. She came to realize that it was really her self-judgment and not the judgment of others that had kept her from progressing into her spiritual mind.

However, Julie still held onto self-rejection as well as the rejection of her brother who had caused her so much pain and grief. She began to ask God how she should feel and think about herself and her brother. Slowly, over time, she began to accept and love herself. She realized that the world's perception of perfection and God's perception (which is about loving self and others the way they are) are completely different. With God's help, she began to regain her self-esteem. This journey brought her peace, self-acceptance, and, eventually, self-love. She began to see life through a different filter. She began reading her scriptures, praying daily, and faithfully attending church again. All of these actions helped her move into the FM station, or her spiritual mind.

The Old Testament talks about looking at the brazen serpent and living, but that few were willing to turn and look *(Numbers 21:9)*. Sometimes the greatest truth is in the simplest act, and yet we are not willing to believe or take the necessary action.

I have attended counseling workshops for the better part of my life and have learned some valuable intervention methods for working with clients. However, it is even more helpful, for those who are able and willing, to look at the brazen serpent—to follow these basic truths—and learn to live in truth and light as they move through their fear mind and into their spiritual mind. Consequently, they become willing to surrender their perception of how they think life should be, and accept life on life's terms and accept God's will for them.

Unfortunately, some clients are unable to accept the family or life situation they were born into. As a result, they are unwilling to take the opportunity to learn and grow from their experiences and their background. One of Satan's greatest tools is shame, including shame of family of origin and who we are. This shame keeps us in our temporal, or fear mind, and in a lower state of consciousness. By accepting and embracing our heritage, past, and losses, we can grow and learn the lessons needed to eventually withstand all things and to rise so we become one with God and His will, in the celestial mind. Often, our relationships with those who live in a telestial state of consciousness teach us life's greatest and most important messages. Opposition in this life is part of God's plan.

As you find peace, love, light, and happiness—no matter your circumstances—you will be attracted and led to others with similar minds. It takes courage, honesty, forgiveness, commitment, and sacrifice to live in this state of mind. It is interesting that these characteristics are also those needed to develop long-lasting relationships. If you want to know what your relationship with God looks like, take an honest look at your relationships with others. It takes courage to admit when you are wrong, and it takes even more courage to accept and forgive others for the way they are. This life is not about trying to change things and others, even the opinions of others when they are less than favorable. If you are still judging others, perhaps you still haven't forgiven yourself. If you can let go and let life happen, think how much energy and time you'll save.

Sylvia's Story

Sylvia struggles with poor body image, and thinks others are judging her harshly as well. Every day she leaves her home feeling fat, even though she is very thin. Food drives her crazy. She has struggled with binging, purging, and restricting since she was fifteen years old. Her family placed a high value on appearance. Her mother and father frequently made negative comments when they saw women who were overweight. Her mother was always dieting and seemed obsessed about the way she looked. Even if her mother had to teach a lesson or had other public commitments, she would cancel at the last minute if she "felt fat."

Sylvia was hospitalized many times for the life-threatening disease called anorexia. She was in a vicious cycle that brought her to a point in her life where she couldn't love herself for who she was. She lived in a fear mind and didn't know how to move to her spiritual mind. She believed so many lies about food and body image that her concept of reality was distorted.

It is my opinion that everything that people do with food is a reflection of their relationships with others. If a person restricts food, perhaps he or she also restricts love, fun, etc. If a person has an unhealthy attachment to food, perhaps he or she has other unhealthy attachments. If a person can't set boundaries with food, he or she, more than likely, has a problem setting boundaries with others.

Sylvia unknowingly allowed her obsession with food and body image to become her god, unwittingly disregarding the commandment, *"Thou shalt have no other gods before me." (Exodus 20:3)*

Sylvia tried to control her life by rigidly restricting her food intake. In reality, her life was so out of control that she almost lost her life. She was finally able to name her eating disorder and realize that it was drawing away her life. She asked me how she could recapture her mind and change her thought patterns. I told her that she couldn't, but God could—and would—if she would let Him. She was hesitant, but came to realize that *she* couldn't fight this battle alone. She was able to identify her wound as deeply ingrained patterns and behaviors that had been passed down from her family of origin.

As she explored the concept of moving through the Eye of the Gethsemane Needle, Sylvia identified her behaviors. She recognized the fear that arose in her Peter-mind. She recognized the self-betrayal in her Judas-mind. She recognized her excessive concern about what others thought of her when she was in her Pontius Pilate-mind. And, she recognized the negative, unrighteous self-judgment that arose in her Mind of the Masses.

In the beginning of our therapy sessions, Sylvia couldn't accept or love herself, but she could keep small commitments. Her first commitment was to keep a food journal and to share the journal with her husband and counselor. She was willing to risk rejection by being completely honest with herself and others. However, what she ended up finding was love and acceptance.

While Sylvia had a rebellious nature most of her life, she now began to surrender her will to someone or something that was greater than she was. As part of the process, she had to forgive all the watchmen in her life who had fallen asleep, including herself and her family. She was also able to forgive herself for the pain she had inflicted upon her body and her family. Not only had she restricted the food in her life, but she had also restricted God and other relationships.

In the telestial state of consciousness, Sylvia could pray only like a child, focusing primarily on her own needs and what she wanted. As she evolved into a terrestrial state of consciousness, she moved into parent-type prayers, dictating her will to God and explaining how He might provide those things that she wanted. Then, as she was able to forgive herself and others and surrender and forsake the world and its lies, she moved into her celestial state of consciousness and began to pray with a more mature understanding and with increased spiritual intelligence. She was willing to surrender her power to God and not to food. Her prayers also evolved as she prayed humbly, submitting her will to God's will. She began to pray for others, including her enemies and those who despitefully used her. She definitely was on the road to recovery and the celestial state of consciousness.

Sylvia knows she is alive today only because of the grace of God. "Let this mind be in you" is now her choice each day. She knows this mind—her spiritual mind—will not betray her unto death. She knows she can trust God. Every day she chooses to live God's laws, she chooses recovery, knowing that only He can change her thinking.

Thought Replacement Therapy

Most people with addictions, such as eating disorders, also have social anxiety. Though Sylvia was initially fearful about attending an eating disorder group, she was willing to risk humiliation, rejection, and the related anxiety created by exposing her shame regarding this disorder and move forward by attending the meetings. As she stepped into the fear, she found that on the other side of fear there was truth, acceptance, and insight. She eventually began to realize that by telling her story, she was able to help others in the recovery process. She came to see that others also had believed the same lies that perpetuated her eating disorder. As she came to accept others as they were, she was better able to accept herself. The thoughts that others would be better off without her were finally extinguished by the truth.

Satan strives to have us believe that his stories, or lies, are really ours. He wants us to take ownership of them. One of my clients explained this tool very explicitly, "Satan made me think that his story was my story." Satan is very adept at getting us to believe that his lies are truth and then having us act upon these lies. It is important to realize that our thought processes include stories and impressions from God, Satan, and ourselves—stories that we have learned and internalized from past life experiences. Some people find the truth to be hard, but some, like Sylvia, find the truth to be healing. If we can identify the source of these stories, we will be able to unravel the truth that will set us free.

It is my opinion that believing a lie for an extended length of time can even lead to a chemical imbalance in the brain. Our thoughts may be more powerful than we realize. This does not mean that people should stop taking medication. No doubt, medication can be an essential part of healing. But, it is also important to nurture only those thoughts and stories that come from God and real truth.

CHAPTER 11
Celestial Rewards

....

Sally describes her personal Gethsemane in the workplace. She explains, "I can honestly say I loved my job and the people I worked with for over sixteen years. I had never complained about any supervisor, I never had to; they were all supportive and acted as advocates." Then things changed. Her next supervisor sought to fortify his own standing by making others look bad. In Sally's case, he searched for, and found, a way to crush her both personally and professionally.

Telestial State of Consciousness

A supervisor who wants to terminate or destroy someone's

reputation can—and does—find fault even when there is no evidence to support his or her accusations. Sally was targeted in this manner by her supervisor who enlisted the help of others to question her competence and ensure her dismissal. His rumors and threats were supported by upper management to preserve a "good company face." No one wanted to admit that he was an out-of-control "bully boss" who zeroed in with laser-like precision to intimidate and destroy people and their careers. Instead of being a supervisor who built people up, he selectively surrounded himself with "yes" people who built him up and inflated his ego.

Sally was contending with the "I need to make you look bad so I can look good" management style. The motive is usually driven by power, greed, pride, and/or jealousy—more directly, the telestial state of consciousness. *"And they have rewarded me evil for good." (Psalms 109:5)*

Satan is the master of deception; he knows how to make bad things look good, and good things look bad. The fact that Satan convinced the masses that Christ and His followers should be destroyed is a perfect example of this phenomenon. I am convinced, however, that in the end, the wheat will be separated from the chaff.

Power to Choose

Our choices give either Satan or God power over our minds. We eliminate Satan's power by putting on the whole armor of God and living by God's commandments. *"Commit thy works unto the Lord, and thy thoughts shall be established." (Proverbs 16:3)*

Do we live in a world that supports lies? Evil took over the minds of the masses as they sought the Savior's blood. How much easier this was than to contend with a Man of Miracles who threatened their power and pride. After all, how could they be wrong after being "right" for so many years? "Kill him!" "Crucify him!" they shouted. No mercy was given to the Lamb of God. Today, these same voices are often heard from the floors of upper management and a variety of other arenas.

"Deliver me, O Lord, from mine enemies: I flee unto thee to hide me. Teach me to do thy will; for thou art my God: thy spirit is good; lead me into the land of uprightness. Quicken me, O lord for thy name's sake: for thy righteousness sake bring my soul out of trouble. And of thy mercy cut off mine enemies, and destroy all them that afflict my soul: for I am thy servant." (Psalms 143:9-12)

Sally felt the piercing injustice of the lies that threatened her sixteen year career. She felt the demoralizing false accusations that wounded her character. She lost her confidence, her reputation, and, ultimately, her job.

Sally was left to carry her burden through the Eye of the Gethsemane Needle, albeit, the liberating phase of her journey. For, through her suffering, she was able to recognize the Savior's loving gesture of peace, as well as meet a critical requirement necessary on her personal journey to become celestial minded. She learned to forgive and accept God's will.

Thought Replacement Therapy

Map Your Personal Gethsemane

To have a personal Gethsemane there must be injustice, betrayal, loss, sacrifice, surrender, and forgiveness—all the elements on the Gethsemane Map.

1. What is the loss or perceived loss?
2. How did you react to the loss?
3. How did the loss impact other relationships?
4. How did the loss impact your relationship with God?
5. How did the loss impact how you feel about yourself?
6. What is the injustice or perceived injustice?
7. What do you need to surrender or sacrifice?
8. What is your will?
9. What is God's will?
10. Who do you need to forgive?
11. Who takes the roles of Judas, Pontius Pilate, Peter, and those who choose Barabbases over the Lamb to be sacrificed?
12. What is your role and theirs?

Every personal Gethsemane becomes an opportunity to draw closer to the Savior, which, of course, places us in a higher state of consciousness, where joy is experienced more abundantly. This, in turn, is mirrored in our relationships with others.

Celestial Rewards

"I am crucified with Christ: nevertheless I live; yet not I, but Christ liveth in me: and the life which I now live in the flesh I live

by the faith of the Son of God, who loved me, and gave himself for me." (Galatians 2:20)

"Blessed are ye, when men shall revile you, and persecute you, and shall say all manner of evil against you. Rejoice and be exceeding glad: for great is your reward in Heaven [mind]: for so persecuted they the prophets which were before you." (Matthew 5:11-12)

After the suffering and eventual forgiveness from betrayal comes the peace, enlightenment, and final resurrection. If we follow the Gethsemane Map, we will be resurrected into this higher state of consciousness, and all things suffered in this life will work together for our good in this life and in the life to come.

"Trust in the Lord with all thine heart; and lean not unto thine own understanding. In all thy ways acknowledge him, and he shall direct thy paths." (Proverbs 3:5-6)

"Honor the Lord with thy substance and with the first fruits of all thine increase: So shall thy barns be filled with plenty, and thy presses shall burst out with new wine." (Proverbs 3:9-10)

"And whatsoever ye shall ask in my name, that will I do, that the Father may be glorified in the Son. And if ye shall ask any thing in my name, I will do it. If ye love me, keep my commandments. And I will pray the Father and He shall give you another Comforter, that he may abide with you forever." (John 14:13-16)

"Then said Jesus, Father, forgive them; for they know not what they do." (Luke 23:34)

CHAPTER 12
A Gethsemane Moment

....

A Gethsemane moment begins with a very small insidious lie or belief that begins to chip away at who you really are. In that moment, you might betray yourself by telling yourself lies. You might be afraid to tell someone the truth for fear they will reject you or use the truth against you. You might remain quiet or run from the truth because it is too painful to deal with.

Perhaps we choose to believe a lie because the truth is too threatening or painful. We want to run and hide so we don't get close to people. Consequently, our shame is covered up with lies. Ultimately, however, the shame bleeds through at every pore until we disclose the truth. The truth is, if we choose to live this life in truth, we will sometimes be rejected by the world, but not by God or disciples of God. God stands up for us when we can't stand up for ourselves.

Thought Replacement Therapy

Paradoxically, there are both those who fear success and those who fear failure. Both groups worry about how they will be perceived by others. They lie to themselves and ultimately believe the lies. Is it possible for one to live in this world and live in total honesty with one's true thoughts? Sometimes people want to be more than who they are, and other times, less than who they are, or, if possible, even invisible, but rarely who they really are. Sometimes they cannot accept being an average person who is afraid to make mistakes. They don't like to feel fear or inadequacy. They have a hard time saying "No," so sometimes, they say, "I can't" and eventually believe they can't. Sometimes they tell themselves, "I can't" and then want to run away from risk or possible failure in the moment. That is where the fight or flight in social anxiety comes from: "Run and hide."

My client, Don, had a strong fear of public speaking. He came from an alcoholic family and was ashamed when he showed emotion. He was taught not to talk, trust, or feel—and to never show emotion publicly for fear of ridicule. Indirectly, he was also taught that what he thought and felt didn't matter. He was not allowed to say "No"; therefore, when he was asked to do something he didn't want to do, he would say, "I can't" instead of "No" or "No, thank you." Sometimes, even when he wanted to do something, he would say, "I can't" because of his fear of things not turning out well. Don had all kinds of irrational fears that crippled his life. He wanted to run and hide, but there was no place to run or hide. Pride separated him from God and then separated him from other people. Pride is synonymous with a lie.

The world has a lotion, potion, and pill for everything—

remedies that oftentimes make us go deeper into the lie. Alcohol paints the awful picture rose-colored. Most of us find it hard to believe when we are lying to ourselves, that God appreciates and loves us just the way we are. However, to have God in our lives requires that we be perfectly honest with ourselves and others. We have to risk rejection of men by relying on full acceptance by God.

Another great loss could include the Mind of the Masses, which waits to destroy self-respect, self-worth, and self-esteem. This destruction of self-respect, self-worth, and self-esteem ultimately separates people from loving God, themselves, or other people. When people do not have a healthy attachment with God they often form unhealthy attachments with other people or attach to addictions. Another loss could also include a waste of time as lost moments turn into lost years. Or, perhaps, other people, places, or things are put before family, which creates another great loss—loss of an opportunity to love or be loved.

When we live out our personal Gethsemane we live in shame and pain. It is then that we want to run and hide. Nothing seems worse than exposing hidden, secret shame. If the lie locks us in this prison of the mind, then, conversely, self-honesty will release us from the shackles of fear, shame and pain. It may become necessary to break the lock on the lie and to divulge the secret to trustworthy individuals. If we break the lie and are rejected, we may want to move away from this judgmental type of personality. Or, is this judgmental personality inside of ourselves? Do we judge ourselves without mercy?

What actions help *you* wake up to the truth?

What actions cause *you* to fall asleep to the lie?

The closer we come to God, the closer we come to spouse, children, friends, and neighbors.

The following story is one example that describes this concept.

I Am Nothing

I have a client, Kelly, who is very high functioning and appears to be very confident in almost every way, with one exception: she believes she is more spiritually mature than emotionally mature.

A few months ago, she came into my office to visit. She told me she was sitting at the breakfast table one day when suddenly and without warning, a convincing thought hit her and seemed to take possession of her mind: *I am nothing*.

Kelly began to find quite a bit of evidence that supported the thought. She related that her sister, a successful businesswoman, had, at one time, been selected as Business Woman of the Year. She also had a very accomplished brother who seemed to do everything right.

Kelly also compared herself with her friends who all seemed to have succeeded in various fields and had accomplished a great deal more, in her mind, than she had. She was nothing. After analyzing and comparing her life with others, she simply realized that she was definitely nothing, and maybe, even less than nothing. That thought continued just long enough to cause her to not want to interact with others because, after all, why would they want to be burdened with someone like her?

A Gethsemane Moment

Kelly was in her Judas or self-betrayal mind. She began to feel fear that others would find out who she really was, so she unconsciously moved into her Peter-mind and denied her feelings and even rejected who she was. The Pontius Pilate-mind was right behind. She began to worry about what others thought of her. It was hard for her to look in the mirror and view herself the way she thought others saw her. The Mind of the Masses came on stage and judged her without mercy, saying she had wasted her whole life, no second chances. Everyone else appeared to win the prize and she was left with nothing, and the game of life was all but over.

Instinctively, Kelly knew it was imperative that she tell God and maybe a trusted friend what she was thinking. A scripture came to her mind, *"Commit thy works unto thy Lord and thy thoughts shall be established." (Proverbs 16:3)*

She prayed fervently that He would change her thoughts. In her Pontius Pilate-mind, she wondered what I would think of her as she shared her experience. There was no pride, just some embarrassment. She seemed to recognize that she had forsaken herself. She was virtually crucifying herself with these negative thoughts.

Fortunately, however, almost as suddenly as the initial thought that she was nothing had entered her mind, from the core of her soul came the inner strength to fight off and reject these counterfeit "realities" that were bombarding her. The moment she surrendered the lie to God and understood the truth, the entire scenario changed. She was able to move into her spiritual mind.

First, Kelly recognized that the thoughts that had held her

captive were all lies. Then she went through the Eye of the Gethsemane Needle and surrendered her thoughts to God. She remembered all of the times God had accepted her offerings, her contributions to life, and how, in fact, in the sight of God, she was not a failure.

Gethsemane Moment Thoughts

Write down the thoughts that crucify you when you deny the truth. Here are some examples derived from the most common lies of the natural man.

In the Temporal/Fear Mind

1. I am not important to anyone.
2. People don't like me.
3. I am not smart enough.
4. Why try? I'll never make it anyway.
5. If people really knew me they wouldn't like me.
6. I am not attractive enough or rich enough.
7. That person would be better off without me, so I better leave.
8. I can't stand to be rejected, so don't get close.
9. Loss of a friendship is too hard, so I won't make friends.
10. I can't stand to make a mistake, so, to be safe, I won't try anything.
11. I was hurt once in a relationship and I can't stand the pain, so it is better not to get close.

12. If I tell him or her truth he or she will reject me.
13. He can't possibly love me as much as he says he does. Or, what is wrong with her for loving someone like me?

How do you resurrect your thoughts or wake up to the truth? Here are some examples. Counter natural man lies with spiritual truth.

In the Spiritual Mind

1. I am important to God.
2. Maybe certain people don't like me, but God likes me.
3. I can do my very best, and with God's help that will be sufficient. I will surrender the outcome to God.
4. I may not be able to make it on my own, but with God's help I will survive.
5. God knows me with all my many flaws and he still loves and forgives me. Maybe someday I can love and forgive myself and every other human being.
6. The world's standards and God's standards are very different. God looks at my heart and not at my worldly status.
7. God needs me to serve Him while I am here, so I need to prepare myself.
8. I love God and want to be as close as I can. I know He will never reject me in spite of all my idiosyncrasies.
9. Do people reject me, or do I reject myself for being honest? The question should be, how does God feel about me? I need to ask God how I should think and feel about myself and others.

10. Maybe someday I can accept and forgive myself for not being perfect. Perhaps, then, I can love myself and feel love from God and other people.

Passage Through Affliction

The passage through affliction can teach us how to take on the mind of the Savior—becoming one with Him and the Father as we forsake the lies that bind us to the temporal/fear mind. It's imperative that we stay awake spiritually—remaining alert as a type of self-watchman in defense against the lies that can originate around us, and even from within ourselves. We must watch, lest we adopt a terrestrial mentality wherein we begin to acknowledge lies based on fear. We will discover the chains that can bind us when we accept our own lies, as well as the lies of others. We will gain a better understanding of how destructive the lies originating in the telestial state of consciousness can be, and how difficult those lies can be to eradicate. We are usually willing to admit to the lie only after a crisis unfolds as a consequence.

It is possible in the terrestrial state of consciousness for us to recognize a lie, feel remorse, and be willing to turn to God and search for a solution.

Lies in a telestial mentality are used by those who wish to elevate themselves—especially in the eyes of the world—and by those who will let their character sink to great depths in order to obtain the false honors they seek. It is difficult for those stuck in the telestial state of mind to acknowledge and admit their situation, but it is not impossible for a person to escape.

Each generation can find the Mind of the Masses that are willing to raise their voice in false witness against the innocent, motivated by a group mentality. Individually, they are not willing to take the time and energy to search for the truth, because it is easier to act according to hearsay, gossip, or popular opinion.

Ultimately, the journey to truth, which is the other side of fear, will bring peace, love, self-acceptance, and insight. Fear is a necessary ingredient for wisdom and growth; however, only by walking through the fear can we overcome the world and move from the temporal mind into the spiritual mind and ultimately a higher state of consciousness.

CHAPTER 13
Thought Replacement Therapy

....

Within the different states of consciousness, we all have different thoughts and actions. In the celestial state of consciousness, we gain freedom. In the telestial state of consciousness, we are held captive and invariably lose our peace of mind. The more truth we believe and embrace, the more we will connect with God and others who live in a similar state of consciousness. Conversely, the less truth we believe, the more disconnected we feel with God and others. There may be a temporary connection with people who live in the telestial state of consciousness, but only for a brief time, and the connection itself is usually a facade. As mentioned previously, we all see life through different filters based on the level of truth or lies we believe.

When life is going the way we want it to, we are probably

living in the celestial or terrestrial state of consciousness. Then, when a test or trial erupts, we are either propelled to the celestial state of consciousness by forgiving, accepting, and surrendering, or we move to the telestial state of consciousness where we try to control and become angry as we blame ourselves or others. When we blame others, it is a natural tendency to want to leave a job, church, spouse, or significant relationship. But, we can only change when we take responsibility for our actions. There is no way we can control the actions of others. Pride can sometimes block reality and keep us from moving into a higher state of consciousness.

Telestial thoughts generate a negative thought process that often separates us from God and other people.

Terrestrial thoughts lift us up, and we say, "I can do it on my own."

Celestial thoughts suggest that we can achieve righteous goals with God's help.

When people live in the celestial state of consciousness, it is because they are able to clear away past debris from their lives. They have powered through shame, blame, and pride, and reached forgiveness, acceptance, and surrender. At this point, the lens in which they view life is pretty clear. They have an increased capacity to love God, themselves, and others.

However, people who live in the telestial state of consciousness struggle with their thoughts. I believe this includes all of us at different times and under different circumstances. Usually, thoughts in the telestial state of consciousness are powered by fear of loss, which causes people to move into a control mode. Here, there may be a need to be "right" at whatever cost. In this state, the individual will bend the truth or do whatever is necessary to be right.

Basically, in the telestial state of consciousness, thoughts are fueled by the desire of being right, looking good, blaming others, controlling others, and, sometimes, doing for others what they could and should be doing for themselves. Basically, taking away another person's free agency, or surrendering their own agency to things of this world.

Here are a few thoughts that fuel the telestial mentality.
- All or nothing thinking is telestial.
- Blaming other people is telestial.
- No hope is telestial.
- Negative thinking is telestial.
- Trying to control other people is telestial.
- Retaliation is telestial.
- Fear that is not based in reality is telestial.
- Inability to forgive is telestial.
- Comparing yourself with others is telestial.

Thoughts and actions that bring you into telestial thinking include pride, guilt, shame, and blame.

Conversely, thoughts that bring love, peace, serenity, and harmony are celestial.
- Thoughts that increase faith and hope are celestial.
- Thoughts that are positive and constructive are celestial.
- Thoughts that inspire are celestial.

Thought Replacement Therapy

Thoughts and actions that bring you into celestial thinking include commitment, forgiveness, surrender, sacrifice, and acceptance.
- Celestial thoughts and actions are based on different degrees of truth.
- Terrestrial thoughts and actions are based on truth mingled with lies.
- Telestial thoughts are based on lies.

Question your initial thoughts or stories by asking;
1. Is it true?
2. How true is it?
3. Is there a higher level of truth?

The following are examples of thoughts that move you into different states of consciousness:

Self-Worth
- Telestial: I can't do anything right.
- Terrestrial: I can love and forgive myself in spite of making a mistake.
- Celestial: God loves and forgives me even though I am not perfect.

Each level indicates an increase of truth that pulls people out of the lie and changes their ability to focus with a clearer perspective of reality.

Forgiveness

- Telestial: I can't forgive my husband for his pornography addiction; if I do, he'll use pornography again.
- Terrestial: I need to forgive my husband for his pornography addiction so I can have peace in my life.
- Celestial: With God's help, I know I can forgive my husband for his pornography addiction.

Can you see how the telestial thought holds you captive? *"To whom ye forgive any thing, I forgive also: Lest satan should get an advantage of us: for we are not ignorant of his devices." (II Corinthians 2:10-11)*

Forgiveness

- Telestial: My husband needs to say he is sorry before I can forgive him.
- Terrestial: I can forgive my husband whether he apologizes or not.
- Celestial: As I forgive my husband, I know that I am being forgiven by God.

Self-Confidence

- Telestial: Things always work for everyone else, but not for me.
- Terrestrial: I believe things can work out for me.
- Celestial: With God's help, I know things can work out for me.

Perseverance

- Telestial: I can't accomplish goals because I am not consistent.
- Terrestrial: In the past, I have not accomplished my goals, but I believe I can accomplish goals.
- Celestial: With God's help, I know I can accomplish my goals.

Self-Image

- Telestial: My happiness comes from my body being perfect.
- Terrestrial: I can be happy whether or not my body is perfect.
- Celestial: God loves me no matter what my body looks like.

Self Image

- Telestial: I don't feel good about myself because of my weight.
- Terrestrial: My weight does not dictate how I feel about myself.
- Celestial: My weight does not dictate how God feels about me. God approves of me no matter how much I weigh.

Taking Responsibility

- Telestial: I am stuck in a situation I don't want to be in.
- Terrestrial: What can I learn from being in this situation?

Thought Replacement Therapy

- Celestial: What does God want me to learn from being in this situation?

Problem Solving

- Telestial: My wife/husband is unreasonable.
- Terrestrial: My wife/husband has the right to be unreasonable. In his/her own mind, he/she is acting in his/her own best interest.
- Celestial: There are no mistakes in God's plan, only learning experiences. Perhaps my wife/husband needs this experience for his/her growth experience in life.

Self-Worth

- Telestial: I am a waste of everyone's time.
- Terrestrial: I am not a waste of anyone's time.
- Celestial: I am a son/daughter of God, and I am not a waste of His time.

Taking Responsibility

- Telestial: I am responsible for other peoples' feelings and actions.
- Terrestrial: I can influence other people, but, ultimately, I am not responsible for their thoughts and actions.
- Celestial: I am responsible for my feelings, thoughts, and actions, and I can love others regardless of theirs. As I surrender my will to God, He can influence my thoughts.

Thought Replacement Therapy

Decision Making

- Telestial: I can't accept my wife's decisions.
- Terrestrial: I think she is making a bad decision, but it is her decision to make.
- Celestial: With God's help, I can accept my wife's decisions and consequences.

Trials and Challenges

- Telestial: I don't trust God because my son is deaf.
- Terrestrial: I think God knows and cares that my son is deaf.
- Celestial: My son has a disability, but God can, and will, make up the difference in my son's life.

Self-Acceptance

- Telestial: If I don't do everything perfectly, I'll never make it in this life or in the next.
- Terrestrial: I can make mistakes and still be okay.
- Celestial: God loves and accepts me in spite of my mistakes

Self-Love

- Telestial: I do not feel like anyone can love me.
- Terrestrial: I know people can love me.
- Celestial: I know God loves me.

Thought Replacement Therapy

Taking Responsibility

- Telestial: Mom and dad don't love me.
- Terrestrial: Mom and dad do love me. They may get angry, but that doesn't mean they don't love me.
- Celestial: I know that God loves me even when mom and dad are upset with me.

Now that you are beginning to understand which pattern of thoughts are telestial, terrestrial, and celestial you may want to ask yourself some questions. First you may want to start a thought journal and begin to record your thoughts or stories and ask yourself certain questions.

To begin with take a personal inventory of your thoughts and/or stories. Analyze your thoughts by putting a feeling by each thought such as hurt, frustrated, insecure, shame, guilt, pride, anxious, fear, peace, love, serenity, etc.

Ask yourself if there was an action that was triggered by the thoughts you are experiencing. Actions might include: control, greed, pride, addictive behaviors, comparing, surrendering, forgiveness, accepting, or not accepting life on life's terms.

Remember you are only a thought away from healing your mind and life. Put each of these thoughts under the celestial, terrestrial, or telestial thought category. Thoughts that heal come and go like waves in an ocean. Thoughts that destroy can become obsessions if you are not careful. They hang on relentlessly, but you must allow them to flow and come and go in their natural course. Every thought is teaching you valuable lessons in life, so this is an opportunity to learn to be mindful of your thinking. The goal is to move from the lie to the truth and not from the truth to a lie. Each higher degree of truth allows us freedom from our own thoughts and each lie holds us captive.

Remember, the war in the heaven/ hell portion of your mind is between the telestial (lie), terrestrial (truth mingled with lies), and celestial (truth) thoughts.

Every choice, thought, and action is irreversibly predicated on a spiritual law that we are either keeping or not keeping in that moment. Each of these are based on intention which is derived from the amount of truth we are able to comprehend.

Our actions, thoughts, and choices either filter in light or filter out light in our mind. Telestial actions and thoughts that come from pride, greed, arrogance, control, etc., often cause you to filter out truth and move into guilt, shame, and addiction. Celestial and terrestrial thoughts and actions help us to take responsibility and be accountable for our actions. These actions and thoughts lead us to greater light and insight within our mind as well as underlying feelings of peace, love, and serenity.

Keep in mind…
1. Celestial: You can see with God's eyes.
2. Terrestrial: You can see with your own eyes and sometimes God's eyes.
3. Telestial: You see with other people's eyes.

When you see with other people's eyes it is usually because you do not trust yourself.

In areas of co-dependency you might experience the following thoughts.

- Celestial: My good feelings stem from being loved and accepted by God.
- Terrestrial: My good feelings stem from being loved and accepted by other people and God.
- Telestial: My good feelings stem from other people, places, and things.

When families are raised with telestial rules such as control, pride, and arrogance, etc., their filter is diminished by lies that are passed down multigenerationally. The following is an example of a family paradigm:
- Telestial thought: I am right even if I have to make you wrong.
- Telestial behavior: I am the head of the household and you need to do what I say.
- Telestial families: Children are taught to be dependent on parents and not on God.

Parents, who want to rule the universe with control, often raise telestial children who see the world through other people's eyes. They don't have a strong sense of self because they were constantly forced to do what the authority in the family told them to do.

Children raised in a telestial family do not learn to make better choices by suffering the consequences of their bad choices. Because their free agency was compromised, they learned from childhood to relinquish their agency to others. A child raised in a controlling, domineering family will follow their parents' behavior into adulthood and either marry a controlling person and be very submissive, or they will become very controlling and domineering themselves.

You have to let go of the lie to achieve the truth. Sometimes it is very difficult to let go of old ways of thinking that have been passed down for many generations. People argue with reality by trying to gloss over and justify the mistake; however, finding the truth can only be accomplished by living certain spiritual laws.

Here is an example of a possible thought process for a client arriving late for an appointment, with the full intent to be on time.

- Telestial thought: I made a mistake and can never be forgiven. I am always late and continue to make the same mistakes. Perhaps, I can never overcome my flaws. The consequence of this thought was a hopeless, helpless feeling.
- Telestial action: Makes up excuses and lies to cover up for lateness: construction, car trouble, lost keys—all lies.
- Terrestrial thought: I made a mistake, but I expect to be forgiven by myself and others.
- Terrestrial action: Client accepts accountability and takes responsibility by apologizing for any inconvenience.
- Celestial thought: God loves and accepts me. With God's help I can overcome my tendency to be late.
- Celestial action: Thoughtfully reconstructs what made her late and makes an honest plan to adjust her schedule.

Through action, accountability, and intention this client was able to move through his/her resistance and arrive at a higher level of thinking.

The last thought instills even more hope and a brighter future, which frees up the person to live in a higher state of consciousness. Thoughts can be very nurturing or very damaging to the psyche. People who primarily live in the telestial state of consciousness do not mature developmentally, emotionally, or spiritually at the same rate as someone who lives in the terrestrial or celestial state of consciousness. Also, since believing lies leads to addictions, most people who live in the telestial state of consciousness tend to use addictions as a form of escape and as a way to self-soothe their negative thoughts, feelings and emotions. There are many addictions in this life, including shopping, alcohol, drugs, money, relationships, pornography, work, food, and sexual addictions, to name a few. All of these addictions provide a distraction from what is real and true.

For example, if a person starts using pornography at fourteen years of age and doesn't stop until they are fifty years old, then, when they do quit, they might be developmentally, emotionally, and spiritually fourteen years old. The addiction and the lies associated with the addiction stunted their growth in those areas.

"Buy the truth and sell it not; also wisdom, and instruction, and understanding." (Proverbs 23:23)

We all have support and resistance in our life, and these come in many different forms; thus, much like the stock market, our self worth and self esteem move up and down in different directions. When the internal voices speak louder than the external voices, we regain our focus on what truly matters.

Often times, the resistance is a belief that keeps us stuck in the story. By staying stuck in the story, one refuses to change a

Thought Replacement Therapy

behavior that affects the belief. If we want to change something in our life, and we come to resistance, if we don't break through the resistance it keeps us stuck in a faulty belief system. Like support and resistance in the stock market, when we "buy the truth" as referred to in Proverb 23:23, we move to a higher state of consciousness where we find wisdom, instruction, and understanding.

Let's look at a diagram that shows the support and resistance.

Telestial

▼ **Fear/pride /control**
I need to be right at all costs.

▼ **Guilt**
I made a mistake and I am not okay.

▼ **Shame**
If I am wrong I must be flawed. Unresolved guilt turns into shame.

▼▼ **Blame/Victim**
How can I be wrong? It must be someone else's fault. I am not happy with my life and feel a need to blame others.

▼ **Addiction/ Obsession**
I need to escape from the world and the pain in the world.

Celestial

▲ **Love/Peace/ Serenity**
You have attached your self-esteem to God's will and these are the resulting feelings.

▲ **Acceptance**
God's will, not mine.

▲ **Surrender**
The outcome is God's business.

▲ **Forgiveness**
Forgiving self and others.

Terrestrial

▲ **Responsibility/ Accountability**
The truth is that I am unhappy with my own life choices.

The lines represent thoughts of resistance and support that keep you stuck in a lower state of consciousness. Or, the thoughts evolve into greater truth as you move through the resistance into a higher state of consciousness.

These above thoughts and actions on the left bring you into bondage of your mind. The thoughts and actions on the right give you personal freedom both in your thoughts and relationships in this life. Incidentally, until you are able to take responsibility and be accountable for your actions, you will not be able to move out of the addictive cycle. One of the first steps in AA (Alcohol Anonymous) is admitting that you are powerless over your addiction and that your life is unmanageable. Until you forgive yourself and everyone else you will stay stuck in telestial thoughts which hold you captive to the lie. Where are you on this matrix and what do you need to do to power through the resistance and move to a higher thought process?

In between the support and resistance is a story we tell ourselves. These stories change over time based on our level of truth, which also changes the filter in our mind or the lens with which we view life. The walls that are built by lies, deception, and denial are brought down and rebuilt by the truth, thus fortifying us from future negative thoughts. The truth really does set you free!

Thought Replacement Summary

CELESTIAL: Thoughts suggest that we can achieve righteous goals with God's help. These thoughts move us into a higher state of consciousness where we are released from the bondage of our mind.

TERRESTRIAL: Thoughts lift us up, and we say, "I can do it on my own and with God's help."

TELESTIAL: Thoughts generate a negative thought process that often separates us from God and other people. These thoughts hold us captive, and we frequently see ourselves as victims.

CELESTIAL: Thoughts and actions are based on different degrees of truth.

TERRESTRIAL: Thoughts and actions are based on truth mingled with lies.

TELESTIAL: Thoughts and actions are predominately based on lies.

Question Each Thought:

1. Is it true?
2. How true is it?
3. Is there a higher level of truth?

Examples:

TELESTIAL: I can't do anything right.

TERRESTRIAL: I can love and forgive myself in spite of making a mistake.

CELESTIAL: God loves and forgives me even though I am not perfect.

CHAPTER 14
The Truth Will Set You Free

....

In almost every presentation I give, people in the audience always want to know how they can live, marry, and work with people who live in different states of consciousness. My first reaction is to tell people that they have been doing it all their lives. The levels have always existed; people just didn't know how to identify them so that they could deal with them. We cannot insulate ourselves from people who live in different levels of consciousness. We cannot live a life avoiding or shunning other people, so we have to learn how to recognize these levels so that we will know how to correctly respond.

Stephanie, a neighbor and friend of mine, recently shared an experience with me. I thought this experience would give people a deeper understanding of the answer as to how to reach that awareness of your own level and the awareness of what level others are on and how to respond. For that reason, and with Stephanie's permission, I decided to share her story.

Stephanie admits that she struggles with terrestrial and, at times, telestial thinking. I believe we all do from time to time. As a friend of mine used to say, if you can "spot it" you have "got it" and I think that is true. I guess, because of my profession, I have never come across *a perfect person or a perfect* family. Problems on different levels occur *within every person and within* every family.

Stephanie was raised in what I would call a dysfunctional family. Her father was an inventor who worked for a major corporation. That corporation took advantage of him and took out patents on a number of his inventions without compensating him for his time and talents. Her father suffered bouts of alcoholism and went from rags to riches to rags many times throughout his lifetime, continually making poor choices. Her parents divorced when she was three years old. Stephanie grew to love and appreciate her mother through all she endured, but she also grew to love and forgive her father in spite of his poor choices. Stephanie states that the older she gets, the more she understands her father's trials. She felt that her early experiences in watching and being a participant in the drama that her father lived helped her to see and understand the different levels that people function in from day to day.

Here is Stephanie's experience that she shared with me, and the thought processes that she went through as she moved from telestial to terrestrial to finally a celestial state of consciousness in dealing with her situation.

During a conversation with Stan, a supervisor with authority over her, Stephanie mentioned that she was experimenting with and developing a procedure that was very effective in helping people. Stan asked her to share what she was doing. She told him that she felt apprehensive about disclosing her idea because she was using this idea in the book she was currently writing and was aware that others in this small work community were also writing books. She added that it wasn't the content as much as it was the way the concept was stated that made it original. He promised that the ideas and concept would be kept confidential.

After reading a rough draft of one of her chapters, Stan indicated that it was original and, offhandedly, said someone might steal it. Stephanie had to admit that comment jarred her. Stephanie asked herself, did he know something she didn't know? What was he implying?

About three weeks later, Stephanie told Stan she was going to be turning her book in for publication shortly. He assured her that he had kept her confidence. However, immediately after making that statement, he handed her his own paper on the same subject, stating his comments the exact way that she had stated hers. While she was reading, he, again, assured her he would keep his commitment to her. Stephanie had given him a key chapter to her book which had an original way of presenting a theory. Stan interjected his own theory in her presentation.

Stephanie's initial telestial reaction was motivated by thoughts of competition that instilled fear in her heart. She wanted to have the opportunity to present these ideas in a form that was original, and that intention seemed lost to her now. He assured her that he would not tell people she stole the presentation from him! This blatant comment made Stephanie's head spin and she found herself at a loss for words. Instantaneously, she gave him complete control of her station tuner and was immediately tuned into the AM station. She watched, as Stan proceeded to distribute his paper to their colleagues, upper management, and what he called his many "followers."

Shocked reaction burst into her mind and heart. How could she have anticipated this action, much less forgive him for such a deep betrayal of her trust? She wasn't sure that she could. Now she was in the "to be seen of men" mentality and the "unrighteous judgment" mentality. Her pride welled up. She wanted to be the first to deliver this idea; after all, she thought of it! Her "Judas-mind" of "self betrayal," kicked into high gear and she was now concerned that her chance for an original presentation was lost forever.

Her next thought was that this individual did this to gain recognition for himself. This stirred up even deeper feelings of betrayal of trust. When she was finally able to compose herself, she told him how she felt. His response was that he thought of these ideas sixteen years ago, but, that he had written them down only three days ago.

To say the least, this only added to the negative feelings she was engulfed in. She was still giving him control of the tuner of her AM station and the volume was intensifying rapidly. As all of this unfolded, it instilled more and more telestial thinking, causing Stephanie to sink into hopelessness and helplessness. She admitted that she was seeing this through other people's eyes and really cared how this would look to others. The more she listened to him, the more she realized he believed what he was saying.

She left and went home. She began to pray about how she should think and feel about Stan and the situation. Suddenly, Stephanie remembered a James Cox seminar she had attended wherein she was taught that nothing is really ours—not our money, our children, our house—all are on loan from God. She was now beginning to regain control of herself and her thoughts by turning to God and facing the situation with her spiritual mind.

After praying, her next thought was that maybe Stan just wrote this to help people. This was more of a terrestrial thought, because now she was seeing it more objectively without judgment, and trying to understand his intention. This thought definitely reduced her fear and increased her understanding. After all, she had always considered this person a friend and it was hard to believe a friend would do something like that. Now, she was seeing this situation with her own eyes as well as God's eyes and she felt a deeper understanding and more righteous judgment.

As Stephanie included God in this very painful process, He began to influence her thoughts and the healing began to take place. Because she began to forgive, she felt more peace of mind.

The next thought was that, perhaps, because he wrote this to help other people, it never occurred to him about the impact this might have on her. This became more of a celestial level of thinking because she was no longer judging, but feeling mercy as she gave him the benefit of the doubt. Since Stan had put his paper in a very powerful matrix, similar to the one that she had showed him, she began to admit that his ideas had some merit and that they worked well with the concept. Once she moved past her own telestial or terrestrial pride, she could see that a lot of what he wrote was true.

Stephanie realized from this experience that she could only get to the celestial level of thinking when she was able to take complete responsibility of the situation, forgive Stan, and surrender the outcome to God, and accept whatever the situation was in that moment. In the celestial state of consciousness, forgiveness is not an option, but a commandment for the righteous purpose of being able to filter in truth and filter out lies. But, forgiving someone does not mean we need to stay connected with them. Perhaps it would be nice if we could, but forgiveness is to keep our connection with God. As a friend once told me, the "we" is about "God and me" and not "you and me."

We live in different states of consciousness and different levels of truth all the time. Sometimes we are off track and not aware of it due to denial, minimization, rationalization, and/or justification. In the early stages of this scenario, Stephanie was derailed by her perceived injustice of Stan's actions. At that point, Stan became the conductor of her train. Stephanie recognized her train was off track because she lost her peace of mind.

To get through the pride and resistance to forgiveness, Stephanie knew she had to take full responsibility for what happened. She had made the choice to show him her work. She had not been coerced into giving him a preview of the work she was going to publish in only a few months; she could have said "no" and still kept his respect.

So what was Stephanie's intention? Was it to look good to her superior? Perhaps she had a little Pontius Pilate going on there.

She admits that "to be seen of men" is quite frequently one of her weaknesses.

After this occurred, Stephanie didn't want to say anything to anyone higher up for fear of retaliation. At that point, she moved into the Peter mentality, where she had to give up what she thought and felt for what people in authority thought and felt.

If we could take this same story and place it on The Gethsemane Map, here is how this story would look:

1. Recognition of a great loss, which included the presentation of an original concept. Writing a book is like giving birth to a baby. She had been in labor for many years prior to the birth of her book.
2. She felt deeply betrayed by a confidant and friend, whether real or perceived, as well as her superior. Truth comes at a high price, even in the lives of good people, as seen in the scriptures.
3. The Pontius Pilate "to be seen of men," in this case, really did matter.
4. It stands to reason that if we can be crucified with Christ we can also be resurrected with Christ. When great trials come into your life it means you are being prepared for a great victory.
5. Ultimately, we have to reach the place of forgiveness, surrender, and acceptance or we will lose our life to years of bitterness. Dennis Ashton, author of "Jesus Wept" said that we will all taste of the bitter cup, but the goal is not to become bitter but better. As Jesus said, "Forgive them for they know not what they do." However, it is good to know that the truth always wins out over time.

6. Surrender your will into God's hands. He is the final judge of all people because only He truly knows their heart and mind.
7. The cost of the Savior's life appeared to be in direct correlation with people believing lies. Ultimately, Jesus gave His life. He was never a victim, but rose above and found the truth that set him free. The victory included being lifted to a higher state of consciousness.

In a like manner, we are not victims but rise from the ashes of sorrow to continually be healed when we surrender our will to God's will.

"But for a small moment have I forsaken thee, but with great mercies will I gather thee." (Isaiah 54:7) This is the path to gain freedom from our thoughts and gain the "Mind of Christ."

This was the perfect victim story. However, if we apply the very principles of celestial thinking and move through the Eye of the Gethsemane Needle, He never allows us to be a victim. It is one of the challenges we have in this life, to move out of the victim role, so we can move to the resurrected role. Our trials and acceptance of our losses make us stronger people. And remember, "we" never have to do this alone. Because celestial thinking causes us to see the story through a different lens, we can move from a telestial story to a celestial story, away from victimhood and captivity of our mind, into freedom of our mind. *"Agree with thine adversary quickly, whiles thou art in the way with him; lest at any time the adversary deliver thee to the judge, and the judge deliver thee to the officer, and thou be cast into prison." (Matthew 5:25)*

The Truth Will Set You Free

This is what I refer to as the prison or captivity of your mind. The progression can advance in the following way:

From

Telestial: My life "sucks."

to

Terrestrial: I can begin to accept my trials in life.

to

Celestial: God goes to great lengths to make celestial people.

Jesus' admonition to all of us is to come follow him on this bitter, sweet road to peace, love, and serenity. One day He will wipe away the tears of injustice and replace them with his mercy. Much of the pain we suffer in this life, we bring upon ourselves, though some of it is not of our own doing. I believe the greatest pain and injustice in our life today is believing lies—both in our own lives as well as living and working around others who also believe lies and perpetuate injustice. Jesus gave everyone their free agency and every experience is a test and a trial of the way we handle that agency. It is not the trial that makes us wise, but the forgiveness of the trial that makes us wise.

Look for the positive in every negative experience. Here is a list of the positive things Stephanie discovered during her trial.

1. The greatest compliment you can give someone is to use their work.
2. Trials can motivate us to action. As Stephanie states, she is a great procrastinator, but she was able to complete this project much faster then she planned. It seemed to catapult her into action.

3. Understanding and application of these principles can increase our awareness and ability to overcome real or perceived injustice in record time. Stephanie admits she is aware that this is only a conversation or a thought away from returning to her initial feelings. She states it was kind of like the effects of food poisoning.

Stephanie is aware that on any given day, her truth can be greater or less, depending on her choices and how she chooses to live her life in the face of adversity. How we accept or reject our trials puts us in either a celestial, terrestrial, or telestial state of consciousness. Again, God goes to great lengths to make us celestial people. Ultimately, every resurrection to a higher state of consciousness requires a deeper level of forgiveness.

"Peace I leave with you, my peace I give unto you: not as the world giveth, give I unto you. Let not your heart be troubled, neither let it be afraid." John 14:2

CHAPTER 15
Real Truth

. . . .

R-Reach for the thought that brought you into your pain or addiction.
E-Examine the truthfulness of the thought.
A-Acknowledge the feelings associated with the thought.
L-Look at the actions that follow the thoughts and feelings.

T-Trust that spiritual inspiration will guide you to a higher level of truth.
R-Respect your truth and others for their truth.
U-Understand what thoughts and actions led to your belief.
T-Turn the thought around and look for higher levels of truth.
H-Hold onto the truth or continue to move to a higher level of truth.

Most addictions and obsessions stem from believing lies. Look at what actions or thoughts either keep you stuck in a lie or bring you closer to the truth.

Here is an example of Real Truth and how it might play out in a real-life scenario:

Reach for the Thought that Brought You into Your Pain or Addiction

Sometimes we reach for a thought like an alcoholic reaches for a drink and we have just as hard a time letting go of the thought as the alcoholic has letting go of a drink. For instance one such thought might be: "Why try? I'll never make it anyway." Or, another common thought would be: "My family deserves someone better than I am." Or, "Perhaps, this is as good as it gets."

Examine the Truthfulness of the Thought

On a scale of 1–10 with 10 being the highest level of truth, how true is your thought?

More than likely, the thought is a 3 or 4 on the scale, or at least, much lower than 10.

Acknowledge the Feelings Associated with the Thought

You might be having the following feelings: "I feel hopeless and helpless." Or, "I feel worthless and disgusting."

Look at the Actions that Follow the Thoughts and Feelings

"I want to give up before I even get started." Or, "I would like to run and hide."

Trust that Spiritual Inspiration Will Guide You To A Higher Level of Truth

Your intuition will tell you that your logic may be flawed. Start thinking a new thought: "I believe that I can have spiritual inspiration that will guide me to a higher level of truth. Perhaps, I should try and leave the outcome to God." If you turn the lie around, more than likely, you will find the truth: "My family does love me. Maybe I do deserve better."

Respect Your Truth and Others for Their Truth

Say to yourself: "I need to accept where I am in the moment so that I can heal and move onto the next level of truth. While I may not agree with other people's truth, I need to accept where they are in the moment as well."

Understand What Actions and Thoughts Led to Your Belief

"Perhaps, I was comparing myself to other people, and I assumed that I could not achieve my goal. Comparing and assuming caused me to believe a lie, which created fear and stopped my progression."

Turn the Thought Around Until You Find Higher Levels of Truth

"I could try. Maybe I will discover important things about myself. If I break through and do the opposite of what the lie tells me to do, maybe my self esteem will increase and, hopefully, my faith." Or, "My family does love and care about me, perhaps, I should love and care about myself."

Hold Onto the Truth or Continue to Move to a Higher Level of Truth

Once you realize the truth, don't slide back or let the negative voices steal the truth. To begin your spiritual fight, live your commitments. Be true to yourself, God, and your fellowman. Remember, when you break a commitment or tell a lie, you open yourself up to believing a lie. Just the opposite is true, when you are honest with yourself, God, and your fellowman, you open yourself up to believing higher levels of truth.

The Twelve Steps of Alcoholics Anonymous have been modified for increased inspiration as we discover the map on our inspired journey into the "mind of Christ."

Step One

"Admit we are powerless over thoughts that make our life unmanageable."

What thoughts bring you in to your pain? Here is an example of one such thought: "I can't forgive myself for not being there for my loved ones. If I had been there, they would not have had to endure such a painful experience." This is the "should of, would of, could of, if only," thought process. This kind of thinking is exceedingly painful and very difficult to eliminate. Another such thought could be: "It doesn't matter if I buy this one expensive item, eat this one extra brownie, or view pornography, just this once doesn't matter. No one will ever know and it doesn't hurt anyone else—just me."

Here is another common negative thought: "Life isn't fair, I have to do it someone else's way, one more time." These are all lies. Look at the actions that follow the thought.

Step Two

"Begin to believe that a power greater than ourselves can remove the thoughts that hold us captive."

The truth could be expressed in the following statement: "I will only eat when I am hungry. It does affect me and other people when I overeat or overspend." In the case of pornography, one might say: "If I view pornography I might begin to objectify women and not live in a world of reality. One consequence is that I might not be satisfied with whom I married and, unconsciously, I could be conveying this to her and that would affect the way she feels about herself and me. Also, viewing pornography will affect my judgment and the way I feel about myself." Or, "Life may not be fair, but I still have my free agency to accept, forgive, or change my situation."

Step Three

"Make a decision to improve our conscious contact with God so He can improve our thoughts."

Through prayerful consideration ask God how we should think, and if our thoughts are true. An example of this could be exemplified in the following question: "Am I eating because I am hungry or out of boredom." Remember the HALT analogy: Don't get too hungry, angry, lonely, or tired.

Step Four

"Make a searching and fearless moral inventory of our thoughts."

Keep a thought journal and be as honest as you can about your current thoughts and how they impact your feelings and actions.

Step Five

"Admit to God, ourselves, and to another human being the exact nature of our thoughts." *"For as he thinketh in his heart so is he."* *(Proverbs 23:7)*

Step Six

"We are entirely ready to have God remove the defects that cause our faulty thinking."

Discover the areas that bring you into the faulty thinking. Was it comparing, assuming, dishonesty, etc. What are your core beliefs? What triggers the faulty thinking?

Step Seven

"Humbly ask Him to remove shortcomings that cause negative thinking patterns."

Pray to find out what thoughts stop your progress or bring you into your pain or addiction. Ask for guidance to overcome negative thinking patterns. *"Commit thy works to the Lord, and thy thoughts shall be established."* *(Proverbs 16:3)*

Step Eight

"Make a list of all persons we had harmed with our negative thinking, including ourselves, and become willing to make amends to them all."

Step Nine

"Make direct amends to such people whenever possible, particularly, ourselves, except when to do so would injure them or others."

Step Ten

"Continue to take a personal inventory of our thoughts."

Step Eleven

"Seek through prayer and meditation to improve our conscious contact with God as we understand Him; praying for His help to remove unwanted thoughts."

Step Twelve

"Having had a spiritual awakening, we give control of our thoughts to God, so He can restore us to the truth."

Remember, we didn't take a train, car, bus, or boat to where we are today, but our *thoughts* and subsequent actions have directed the course.

As we practice these principles in all our affairs, we will be guided back to the FM station where we will find real truth. We will no longer be held hostage by our thoughts.

In this life we may lose our worldly possessions, our loved ones, our health, and even our reputation. *"But who has known the mind of the Lord, that he may instruct him? But, we have the mind of Christ." (I Corinthians 2:16)*

Thought Replacement Therapy

The Twelve Steps are reprinted and adapted with permission of Alcoholics Anonymous World Services, Inc. ("AAWS") Permission to reprint and adapt the Twelve Steps does not mean that AAWS has reviewed or approved the contents of this publication, or that AAWS necessarily agrees with the views expressed herein. A.A. is a program of recovery from alcoholism only - use of the Twelve Steps in connection with programs and activities which are patterned after A.A., but which address other problems, or in any other non-A.A. context, does not imply otherwise. Additionally, while A.A. is a spiritual program, A.A. is not a religious program. Thus, A.A. is not affiliated or allied with any sect, denomination, or specific religious belief.

THE TWELVE STEPS OF ALCOHOLICS ANONYMOUS

1. We admitted we were powerless over alcohol—that our lives had become unmanageable.
2. Came to believe that a Power greater than ourselves could restore us to sanity.
3. Made a decision to turn our will and our lives over to the care of God as we understood Him.
4. Made a searching and fearless moral inventory of ourselves.
5. Admitted to God, to ourselves, and to another human being the exact nature of our wrongs.
6. Were entirely ready to have God remove all these defects of character.
7. Humbly asked Him to remove our shortcomings.
8. Made a list of all persons we had harmed, and became willing to make amends to them all.
9. Made direct amends to such people wherever possible, except when to do so would injure them or others.
10. Continued to take personal inventory and when we were wrong promptly admitted it.
11. Sought through prayer and meditation to improve our conscious contact with God, as we understood Him, praying only for knowledge of His will for us and the power to carry that out.
12. Having had a spiritual awakening as the result of these Steps, we tried to carry this message to alcoholics, and to practice these principles in all our affairs.

Copyright, A.A. World Services, Inc.

About The Author

Cynthia Hunt was born in Southern California. Her daughter, Heather, and son-in-law Bert, have blessed her with two wonderful grandsons.

Cynthia has worked as a clinical therapist for the past 20 years, accumulating approximately 30,000 face-to-face contact hours with clients. She has a private practice and specializes in depression, anxiety, abuse, dysfunctional family and relationship issues, as well as eating disorders, pornography, and substance abuse.

Cynthia received her Master of Social Work degree from Our Lady of the Lake University in San Antonio, Texas. She received her Bachelor of Science degree from Utah's Westminster College, and graduated from the Certified Addiction Counselor program at the University of Utah. Of all the schools she has attended, she states that the greatest has been the "school of life."

Cynthia's goal in writing this book is to provide a tool to open the spiritual eyes of her readers. It is her hope that the understanding obtained from this book will allow readers to find a forgotten state of peace, joy, and understanding.

Cynthia Hunt is still seeing clients in Salt Lake City, Utah. If you would like to schedule an appointment or for speaking engagements, please e-mail her at cynthialcsw@comcast.net or call (801) 355-5888. You may also visit www.thoughtreplacementtherapy.com.